*THE A. S. W. ROSENBACH FELLOWSHIP
IN BIBLIOGRAPHY*

STANDARDS OF
BIBLIOGRAPHICAL DESCRIPTION

PUBLICATIONS

STANDARDS
OF
BIBLIOGRAPHICAL
DESCRIPTION

by

CURT F. BÜHLER
JAMES G. McMANAWAY
LAWRENCE C. WROTH

Rosenbach Fellows in Bibliography

UNIVERSITY OF PENNSYLVANIA PRESS

Philadelphia
1949

Copyright 1949

CONTENTS

INTRODUCTION

AS Dr. McManaway points out elsewhere in this volume, it is some twenty years since the late R. B. McKerrow published his *Introduction to Bibliography for Literary Students,* a work which since its appearance has modified entire aspects of literary scholarship. That the volume set forth standards of bibliographical research which have revolutionized not only the methods of the bibliographer but of the literary historian as well will not be questioned. Embodying ideas and methods which have forced a reëxamination of earlier assumptions, it has led literary students to revise many of their beliefs regarding the nature of texts and editions which hitherto had been based largely on aesthetic grounds. Though McKerrow's book was certainly not created *in vacuo* but is the expression of ideas and principles worked out in contact with other scholars, nevertheless it is now clear in retrospect that its appearance marked an epoch in the history of modern literary scholarship.

Yet, great as the influence of McKerrow and his contemporaries has been, the bibliographer today is still faced with the predicament that there are neither standards nor forms of bibliographical description which have found general acceptance. Current practice varies greatly from period to period and from field to field, and even within a limited period and field it cannot be maintained that agreed standards have been achieved. It was with a view to raising basic questions of theory, objectives, and methods, and to contributing to the formulation of acceptable standards that the 1946-47 series of lectures under the A. S. W. Rosenbach Fellowship in Bibliography was planned.[1]

In a departure from the earlier practice of having a single lecturer for the series, three distinguished bibliographers were in-

[1] The timeliness of the subject is illustrated by the fact that there has now been announced for publication by the Princeton University Press a volume by Fredson T. Bowers entitled *Principles of Bibliographical Description.*

vited, each of whom was identified with a distinct and significant field. It was confidently believed that we should thus get three separate approaches to what must surely be common problems, but the extent to which there would be agreement as to best, or standard, solutions could appear only after the lectures had been delivered. In any case, a separate examination of the problems by bibliographers of great eminence could not fail to produce valuable results, even were complete accord not achieved.

The three fields selected, namely fifteenth-century printed books, English literature to the close of the seventeenth century, and early Americana, all present specific problems which have occupied scholars and collectors alike, both in this country and abroad, for a long time, yet without the emergence of satisfactory solutions or agreed standards. It must be acknowledged that while there is much common ground among the papers here presented, there is still diversity. The authors are united in their sincere belief in the importance of bibliography both for itself and as a tool of research, but their experience, based upon a great variety of materials derived from different times and lands, has, as was doubtless to be expected, not brought them to complete agreement on a good many points.

Nevertheless, the variety of opinions expressed will surely not disturb the reader if he accepts, as he ought to do, Bühler's basic dictum that "it is not wisdom to compel all scholars to employ the same set of rules." The original planners of the present Rosenbach series had no thought of so doing. What they were interested in was not uniformity but an advance toward acceptable minimum standards. They would not now maintain that even this limited objective has been wholly achieved, but that important progress has been made toward it they confidently believe.

John Alden

INCUNABULA

CURT F. BÜHLER
The Pierpont Morgan Library

INCUNABULA

Curt F. Bühler

THE subject for discussion is a problem which, to the literary student, would appear first to have been approached three centuries ago[1] and which some scholars may consider to have been solved, in all its broadest aspects, 175 years later. When in 1826 Ludwig Hain issued the first volume of his *Repertorium bibliographicum*[2] he established the foundations for bibliographical descriptions of incunabula, which, with only minor alterations and those additions that the passing years have inevitably brought forth, are still in use today. His bibliographical descriptions came to be amplified within fifty years by the systematization of type analyses,[3] leading ultimately to the works of Proctor[4] and Haebler,[5] and were further implemented twenty-five years ago through the technical investigations of Ronald B. McKerrow,[6] his colleagues and successors. These modifications and refinements have been fully utilized by the two most representative systems—the British Museum Catalogue of fifteenth-century books,[7] and the *Gesamtkatalog der Wiegendrucke*[8]—but the basic tradition may by now be called venerable and its principles so thoroughly entrenched that few radical innovations can be expected to meet with much approval from the worldwide group of specialists in this field.

A difficulty which should be recognized at the outset is that incunabulists have, in general, pursued their own sets of rules and standards and have ignored the dicta of their colleagues in other branches of bibliography. No matter how slight one's acquaintance with the standard incunabula bibliographies may be, it is no doubt apparent to everyone that incunabulists have blithely overruled all the elaborate regulations for describing books laid down by the American Library Association[9] and kindred organizations. The wisdom of this—or the lack of it—is not for me to judge, but it is a fact which cannot be overlooked. The explanation for it is simple.

It must always be borne in mind that incunabula represent the bridge between manuscripts and the printed books of the sixteenth century (these being, to all intents and purposes, the identical objects we are familiar with today)—and as they thus stand between the handwritten book and the modern printed volume, they partake of the problems of both. On the one hand, the heterogeneous nature of the contents of many fifteenth-century printed books is characteristic of the medieval manuscript *Sammelband;* the anonymity of many of the early printers is paralleled by that of the scribes; and the frequent absence of title-pages, indices, tables of contents, and so forth, brings to mind the similar omission of such information in the manuscripts of the same period. Thus, in the textual description of an incunable, certain usages employed for the catalogues of manuscripts have been necessarily retained. On the other hand, in the practical machining of the book, the fifteenth-century volume differs but little, if at all, from those books produced in the following three centuries. But here too, the incunable often preserves practices more readily identified with the scribe.

Nevertheless all bibliographers are agreed that certain details belong to every bibliographical description —certainly the name of the author, the title of the work, the place of origin, the printer, and the approximate date —and yet these are the precise points where the makers of incunabula descriptions most often depart from the usage of their colleagues interested in later books. In the matter of verbatim reproductions of title-pages, where these occur, or of specimens of text, of type analyses, of descriptions of illustrations and of decorative initials, of identification and explanation of variant settings—in all such bibliographical niceties, the incunabulist is, speaking generally, at one with the bibliographer of early English and American imprints.

Before turning to the bibliographical descriptions themselves, it is, I think, necessary to determine exactly what we mean by bibliography and the purposes for which such descriptions may be intended. For the former I can do no better than to quote the enlightening definition recently given by Dr. Greg:[10]

For in the ultimate resort the object of bibliographical study is, I believe, to reconstruct for each particular book the history of its life, to make it reveal in its most intimate detail the story of its birth and adventures as the material vehicle of the living word. As an extension of this follows the investigation of the methods of production in general and of the conditions of survival.

Nor would I, in common with the expressed opinions of Dr. Pollard and Sir Stephen Gaselee,[11] entirely exclude enumeration or compilation from the purview of this discipline. The late Keeper of Printed Books in the British Museum has sensibly written:

Whether such enumeration is a process in a science or not has never greatly troubled me, so long as it is done in a scientific spirit. It is essential work, and long usage has decided that the man who does it is called a bibliographer.

Perhaps it may also be fitting to recall Copinger's classic observation that bibliography is "the grammar of literary investigation,"[12] certainly the briefest, and, to my way of thinking, possibly the happiest, of the definitions.[13]

As to the ultimate purposes for which the descriptions might be made, these may be several, but whether they be designed for a full-length descriptive bibliography, say of some press or of a particular author, or for a more general catalogue of some collection or of some special subject, it is likely that the basic pattern will be pretty much alike in every instance. Particular details, it is true, will be more emphasized in one instance than in another, but the over-all description, it is safe to say, will remain very much the same.

Various rules for such descriptions—all of them admirable for their specific purposes—have been compiled; we have, for example, those propounded by the British Museum,[14] Guppy,[15] Klebs,[16] Polain,[17] Delisle,[18] Duff,[19] Cowley,[20] and others.[21] As Dr. Pollard, it is said,[22] wisely observed: "It does not much matter what form you give to your bibliographical statement provided you make your intentions perfectly clear." If, then, I shall rely chiefly upon the *Gesamtkatalog*,[23] it is not so much because I feel that this work surpasses the others in suitability, but rather because the *Gesamtkatalog's* rules are unquestionably serviceable, because they were formulated only after many years of patient study and trial effort and because, a consideration of especial importance for incunabula, they are international in origin and in scope.

The books that were printed in the fifteenth century readily fall into two groups for the purposes we have in mind: those that have already been correctly described at length, and those that have not received such treatment. The former group, once the British Museum's volume of French incunabula (now, I believe, in press) makes its appearance, will easily include ninety per cent of the extant editions produced in the fifteenth century. The latter small group will probably not contain editions of very great literary or historical import; and, since they have not been adequately described in three hundred years of search for such books, it is entirely likely that they are either unique or are known in but a very few copies. These differing groups should, in my opinion, be differently treated in the bibliographies of the future.

In view of the fact, then, that most incunables have been so adequately described, I am not at all sure what purpose a full-length bibliographical description with quasi-facsimile reproductions of large sections of text is expected to serve. Naturally any catalogue containing satisfactory details for the bibliographer will include, as a minimum, those to be found in Collijn's catalogues[24] —that is: author, title, place, printer, and date, followed by a list of references to bibliographies where a full description may be found.[25] This will surely satisfy any bibliographer as far as identification of edition is concerned.

For the analytical bibliographer, however, it would be practical—and, indeed, desirable—to supplement the heading (or general bibliographical notice as used by Collijn and the Italian *Indice*)[26] by what one may call a collational heading. This would include, among such other details as the case may require, the format, the number of leaves, the quires and signatures, foliation or pagination, the "make-up" (that is, types, initials, illustrations, etc.), and the particulars as to the general appearance of the printed page.[27] These details would, subject to those modifications which will be mentioned later on, follow the precepts of the *Gesamtkatalog*. To include such matters, omitted by Collijn and the *Indice*, is advisable from several points of view. It would, for example, supply the strictly analytical bibliographer with those items of information which he requires for his technical analysis of the physical composition of the volume without necessitating reference to any other work. At the same time, the inclusion of such information would neither prove onerous for the printer nor prohibitive for the publisher.

In my opinion anyway—and this applies also to palaeography—bibliography is not so much an end in itself as it is an ancillary investigation to the study of the text (be it literary, historical, or scientific);[28] consequently, it seems to me that a complete account of the textual contents of any volume (what Klebs called "the literary collation") is absolutely required. In short the bibliographer, and in the long run the historian of culture for whom the bibliographer is laboring, expects to be informed of three basic facts: (1) what edition does the book belong to, (2) what are the principles of its physical construction, and (3) what does the volume contain.

As I see it, the reproduction in facsimile of large portions of text in the case of incunabula already fully described is unnecessary, redundant, and without value. Let us take, for example, the first edition in Greek of Aristotle's works as printed by Aldus. It can hardly be called a rare book since the new *Census*[29] lists forty-three American copies in varying states of completeness. The standard bibliographies describe this edition in full. Hain (No. 1657) and the British Museum Catalogue (V:553-558) each devote more than 125 lines to their descriptions of it and in the *Gesamtkatalog* (No. 2334) this is extended to four columns and 232 lines. While Mlle Pellechet[30] contented herself with thirty-nine full-page lines, M. Polain (No. 289) needed four pages and 197 long lines to complete his analysis. It may indeed be said that this work has been sufficiently often, and sufficiently minutely, described to serve all conceivable demands for the identification of edition.

Or, for another example, let us consider the well-known Cologne Chronicle. This may certainly be called a common book for there are twenty-seven copies in this country and the *Gesamtkatalog* counts 115 before adding "und zahlreiche andere." Yet there are at least twenty bibliographies,[31] six of which are inevitably consulted in the preparation of any catalogue or bibliography of fifteenth-century books, that offer a description with diplomatic reproductions of text sufficient, at the very least, for the purposes of identification.

Any bibliography, or any catalogue pretending to contain bibliographical descriptions, should, in my opinion, omit such quasi-facsimile reproductions of text as are readily available in the standard books of reference. Such textual specimens serve no scholarly purpose, since edition has been established by earlier bibliographies; to print these identical passages in future bibliographies is an entirely uneconomic waste of time, paper, and ink. On the other hand, it seems quite obvious that *any* deviations from the standard descriptions noted in *any* of the copies examined require meticulous and exhaustive annotations.[32] Whatever variations may come to the investigator's attention should be explained, wherever possible, in the light of the printing practice or editorial responsibilities of the day. The time, trouble, and expense involved in the presentation of quasi-facsimile reprints of texts available elsewhere could, and should, be turned to the much more useful pursuit of thorough textual examination and minute comparisons of several copies.

But for incunabula already described *in extenso* in the standard bibliographies, there are still problems requiring investigation on the part of the bibliographer, cataloguer, or compiler. These problems center largely on questions of author and title, probably the most difficult and confusing uncertainty facing the incunabulist. In view of E. P. Goldschmidt's[33] recent and excellent exposition of this problem, it may seem unnecessary to add any further examples. But this much needs to be said. Although the *Gesamtkatalog* has undertaken considerable research with a view to establishing author and title, these notations are not always correct.[34] More irritating than this is the fact that each of the standard bibliographies pursues its own course, often to the utter confusion of the literary student, as to author and title,[35] though it must be admitted that in many cases cross-references are supplied and, on occasion, quite liberally. Again it happens that sometimes within the same institution, the headings of the special incunabula catalogue differ in their ascriptions from those found in the other catalogues of that institution. Thus in the British Museum[36] the same work will be found under one author and title in the general catalogue, under another in the incunabula catalogue and, possibly, under a third in the various catalogues of the manuscript collections. This may perhaps be forgiven because of the special nature of fifteenth-century books, but it is surely not too much to ask that the same work be consistently entered in the same way throughout *one* catalogue. Unfortunately such uniformity is not invariably found, and this is specifically true of that otherwise entirely admirable catalogue of the fifteenth-century books in the British Museum.[37] The establishment of the correct author[38] and title should be one of the chief duties of the bibliographer of incunabula, and a bibliography which fails to do so can hardly be viewed as entirely satisfactory.

The bibliographical description for the sort of books we have been discussing should, then, contain a general heading, a collational heading, and a list of the literary contents of the volume. This ought to be followed by a section of notes and annotations to explain technical problems when they are encountered in the book and, where necessary, a detailed study of the illustration, as well as particulars connected with the transmission of the text. The extent of such notes and annotations will largely be governed by the nature of the book under examination; a late edition of a popular short book, such as the *Cordiale,* will probably present few problems in printing technique, and the nth edition of the *Doctrinale* or of the Bible will require little literary discussion.

This section of notes and annotations promises, however, to play a progressively important role in the future bibliographies and catalogues of incunabula. If I may be permitted to allude to a book in my own library, this will, I think, fairly illustrate the important evidence which textual examination,[39] for example, may present in support of bibliographical theory. The volume I have in mind belongs to the edition described by the *Gesamtkatalog* under No. 8387 and it is there listed—unfortunately not very correctly[40]—as an Italian translation of the "Lives of the Philosophers" by Diogenes Laertius. The book was printed at the Florentine press of Bonaccorsi and Francisci on the 5th of July 1488.

My copy, at first glance, seems quite perfect and agrees throughout with the full descriptions given by GW, BMC (VI:671), Hain-Reichling[41] (6207) and Pellechet (4281). The volume has the required seventy folios (signed a-h⁸ i⁶), is printed throughout in type 1:110R of these printers, and is similarly set up throughout the volume. Various papers were used in the production of this edition, but that sort found, for example, in signature "f" has the same watermark as the paper of quire "d." The first leaf of each gathering[42] also bears the manuscript notation "filoxofi," a Venetian dialectal form indicating that each quire should belong to this edition of the *Vita de philosophi*.[43] Thus far the volume seems perfectly normal. Save by reading through it, however, there is absolutely no way to discover exactly what is the matter with my copy, but once one does so, it immediately becomes apparent that quire "f" does not belong to this book at all but forms part of the same printer's edition of Phalaris' Letters (also in Italian) produced by this press less than two months earlier (17 May 1488).[44]

The printing-house practice thus becomes plain to the investigator. It is self-evident that this firm did not bind its books as soon as the sheets were sufficiently dry to do so; if they had, this misbinding could not possibly have occurred. Again, it is equally evident that the books were not stored as complete unbound copies, for in such circumstances my copy would have been perfect. The "filoxofi" at the beginning of the quires clearly shows that the unbound sheets were stored as separate gatherings; through some slip in the storeroom, the wrong clue-word was written at the top of this particular quire. When my book came to be bound, the binder picked up a gathering from each of the nine piles labeled "filoxofi" and thus the wrong signature "f" found its way into my copy.

The examination of the textual contents of this copy,

then, throws some interesting side-lights on the methods of book production by a characteristic Florentine firm of the fifteenth century.

While the artistic and decorative aspects of the cuts, borders, and initials found in incunabula have been the subject of considerable research, the evidence which such decorations may afford as to printing technique or transmission of text does not seem to have been investigated with sufficient thoroughness. It may be possible—particularly where a cut is employed a number of times—to discover the order in which the forms passed through the press. Also, as happens not infrequently, the same cut may be found both in the inner and outer forms of the same quire. This would be evident proof that simultaneous printing of inner and outer forms on two presses, with the intention of perfecting when half the copies of each had been printed off, did not take place.[45] Again, the cuts themselves are useful in establishing the chronological listing of the undated products of a press, or in the dating of various editions. Dr. Pollard has shown what can be accomplished along these lines in his account of the woodcuts used for the various *Horae* printed by Philippe Pigouchet.[46]

The transfer of blocks, and the copying of them, has also claimed the attention of students, but in the main these scholars have confined themselves to the book productions of only a single country. This study could, I believe, be profitably extended over the entire field of fifteenth-century printing, and the international exchange of such cultural mediums brought out afresh.

Such investigation seems to lie more within the province of the bibliographer than in that of the art historian.

A case in point, for example, is the story of the cuts in that collection of fables known as *Bidpai* or the *Directorium vitae humanae*.[47] The first edition of this book was produced by Conrad Fyner in Urach about the year 1481 (Copinger 1360)[48] and contained 127 woodcuts. Shortly thereafter Fyner issued a second edition (Hain 4028) differing from the first in having but 123 cuts (by repetition 126). The blocks then passed into the hands of Johann Prüss in Strassburg; his Latin edition (Hain 4411) of *circa* 1490 included only 114 different illustrations,[49] nine blocks having apparently never reached him. So much, in part at least, has been known for many years, but further investigation shows that the evidence of the woodcuts is important for the study of the transmission of the textual contents as well.

A curious misprint in Fyner's first edition enables us to state with certainty that the Prüss edition was modeled upon the first—not the second—of Fyner's editions. On folio 62 verso of the first edition the cut is printed upside down, an error corrected on folio 54 recto of the second. Prüss, however, seems to have had the earlier Fyner edition before him when he was planning his volume, for in the Strassburg edition this cut is also incorrectly inverted as in the *editio princeps*.

Later in the century two illustrated Spanish editions of *Bidpai* made their appearance. The earlier of these, produced by Pablo Hurus in Saragossa in 1493 (Haebler 340),[50] I have unfortunately been unable to see. The second was printed by Friedrich Biel in Burgos nearly five years later (Haebler 341); two copies of this edition are in the Pierpont Morgan Library.[51] The Hurus edition, according to the information supplied by Kurz's *Handbuch*,[52] is certainly based on German models; I cannot, unfortunately, be more specific. In turn, Biel's edition, whether or not a reprint with different cuts of the Saragossa one, can be certainly shown to be based (directly or indirectly) not on the Prüss but on the Fyner editions and specifically on the earlier of these. That Biel did not follow the Prüss edition is certain, since the Burgos book contains copies of cuts not found either in Prüss's volume nor in the Fyner reprint. Furthermore, the cut which was inverted in the *editio princeps* also appears that way in Biel's edition. Clearly, therefore, the Spanish edition by Biel descends, directly or indirectly, from the first Urach edition and not from any of the eight later ones, in German and in Latin, printed in Germany before 1490.[53] Illustrations, then, can be successfully used as evidence in the application of the "genealogical method" for establishing family relationships between printed volumes, as Lachmann has employed this method for the study of manuscripts.[54]

We have thus every reason to believe that the section of notes and annotations will in the future include such accounts of printing practice and technique as will materially increase our knowledge of the production methods of fifteenth-century publishing houses.

At the very end of the bibliographical descriptions for those incunabula that have already been sufficiently identified, it will be necessary for analytical bibliographers to record the copies examined and a selection of those

known to be in other libraries. In the case of bibliographical analyses designed for catalogues, it is essential, in
addition to whatever details there may be relating to
provenance, to note the size and the binding of the copy.
For the bindings themselves, annotations of a bibliographical nature may be necessary. Much has been
written, it is true, of their artistic and heraldic character
but, as Dr. Greg (*Studies*, p. 26) has so aptly put it,
"of the technical aspects of binding, the actual gathering,
sewing, forwarding, and covering, we still know next
to nothing historically." Here much research remains
to be done.

And thus, I believe, we have covered all the details
needed for an adequate bibliographical description of
those incunabula already well known and described at
full length in the standard works bearing on this subject.

When, however, we turn to that group of books for
which no adequate description is available, or where
whatever is available is grossly inadequate, the bibliographer is obliged to describe the book in full. Since, at
one time or another, he will undoubtedly have to list
both described and undescribed incunabula together, it
is certainly desirable that the arrangement of the descriptions be identical throughout. The chief and indeed
the only difference between the two groups will be that
for the undescribed books a quasi-facsimile reproduction
of sections of text will follow the collational heading.
Uniformity can be achieved within a work containing
both sorts of incunables by following the outline set
forth by the *Gesamtkatalog*. For the detailed notes on

specific copies, the suggestions offered by Guppy or the British Museum Catalogue will serve admirably. There are, however, a few modifications of the *Gesamtkatalog's* rules which I should like to suggest for your consideration; they will be referred to in the order in which they occur in the preface to volume III.[55] Obviously wherever German forms or interpolations are introduced, these would be rendered in English in our bibliographies.

The rules for the general bibliographical note are reasonably satisfactory, except that it is pointless, as I view it, to reproduce here the date as it appears in the original form.[56] I should prefer to find in the heading only the modern equivalent; the original date will, of course, be reproduced in its proper place in the textual description. I am also not at all happy about the *Gesamtkatalog's* decision to include a note as to the format—that is, the folding of the sheet—in the general bibliographical notice; it seems better to place it at the beginning of the collational heading. After all, the format does not help to identify the edition, except possibly as to size.[57] There are, for example, three undated Bibles[58] printed by Eggestein between 1465 and 1470 and a similar number produced by Nicolaus Götz about 1478,[59] but they are all folio volumes, so that a notation as to folding will certainly not serve to distinguish one edition from another. The format, it seems to me, belongs more logically in the section devoted to the physical make-up of the book.

The bibliographical references which may apply to this sort of book can be suitably placed immediately below the heading, forming a new paragraph. It must readily be admitted that this is not, perhaps, the ideal position for such notations, but there are two strong arguments in favor of this arrangement. First of all, placing the references here corresponds to the practice suggested for the adequately described incunabula; having no text reproductions for the identification of edition, these require that such information be supplied in a conspicuous place. Secondly, it is quite likely that no earlier bibliographical reference for the book is known. On the other hand, if the book has been previously and incorrectly described, it is highly probable that such a description will be found in but one—certainly in but a few[60]—of the standard books of reference. Thus this paragraph will not, in any case, be a very extensive insertion. For the sake of uniformity, then, it is worth recommending that the bibliographical references be left directly below the general heading, a practice sanctioned by no less a bibliographer than Isak Collijn.[61]

The collational heading can, in turn, be improved by several minor alterations. Though the *Gesamtkatalog* does not invariably do so, it seems to me a useful bit of information to supply the exact position of blank leaves in the book, both by count and by signature.[62]

Again, instead of providing the unsigned gatherings of an entire book with alphabetical sequences of twenty-three roman letters enclosed within square brackets, I would suggest that such quires be identified by arabic numbers also bracketed. Traditionalists need not be too disturbed by this suggestion since it was employed with complete success even in the fifteenth century. Such

printers as Hamann, Renner, Arrivabene and Torresanus (in Venice), Koberger (in Nuremberg), Amerbach, Meister and Kollicker (in Basel), and, last but not
least, William Caxton (in Westminster), successfully
signed gatherings with arabic numbers.[63] In the case of
manuscripts, quire numberings of this sort were used by
Montague Rhodes James[64] in his many catalogues, and
for incunabula descriptions they have been employed by
Polain, Collijn, and Seymour de Ricci.[65]

A full alphabet, of course, presents no problems, and
a collation a-z is easily recognized as describing twenty-
three quires. To incunabulists of mathematical aptitude,
perhaps, less than a full alphabet or more than one may
present no obstacle, and for them a-o is just as simple as
1-14. But for myself, I must confess that I am forever
counting the letters of the alphabet on my fingers and
regretting that I have but ten of them. The use of
arabic numbers would avoid such a difficulty. Indeed, it
would obviate another cause for confusion. Occasionally
the British Museum Catalogue and the *Gesamtkatalog*[66]
begin their alphabets at different places in the same book.
The BMC, for example, may assign an arbitrary symbol
to a quire of preliminary matter where the GW uses the
first letter, and so quire [a] in one bibliography will not
correspond to quire [a] of the other. If numbers are
used, it would, of course, only be sensible to label the
first gathering as [1]. Naturally, if the book is partly
signed and partly unsigned, it would be necessary to
supply the unsigned gatherings with such signatures as
will conform to the rest of the book.

Although the controversy raised by Consentius[67] regarding the evidential value of types may have left a lingering doubt in the minds of some scholars, we can surely all agree that the listing of the types used in a volume is sufficiently useful to be retained. If it does nothing else, such practice aids in the visual reconstruction of the appearance of the volume, and for that purpose I would suggest that instead of merely listing the types as the *Gesamtkatalog* does, they should be identified as to the manner in which they were employed. The BMC[68] occasionally is very specific in this respect, and such special information has a justifiable place in bibliographical descriptions. At the other extreme—and this is a practice I can hardly recommend—stands the catalogue of the English incunabula in the John Rylands library. Contrary to Guppy's specific suggestions, as expounded in his *Rules*, the only notation as to type included in this catalogue is the remark "black letter." Since all the books there listed, I think without exception, were printed in black letter, this note is hardly very informative.

The only other item in the collational heading which, to my way of thinking, requires amplification concerns the note as to the possible illustrations found in an incunable. Such a note as "46 woodcuts" means nothing, whereas "45 different (1 repeat) woodcuts by Dürer here used for the first time" (*Ritter vom Turn*, Basel, 1493—H15514—a copy of which is in the Pierpont Morgan Library) would convey a great deal of important information. So short a note (as is found in Manuel Díaz, *Llibre de menescalia*, Saragossa, Hurus, 6 May 1495—GW 8287)as "25 woodcuts" might be extended with greater intellectual honesty to read "13 woodcuts, by repetition 25, all but the first previously used in Haebler 160."[69] If the details are too lengthy, they must, of course, be placed among the notes, as has already been suggested, but a short accurate account properly belongs in this paragraph.

The textual description—that is, reproductions from the textual contents for the purpose of identification—should follow immediately upon the collational heading. Here, I should most emphatically recommend that all faces of type be reproduced in roman. The practice of some North European[70] bibliographers, not endorsed by the British incunabulists,[71] is to reproduce gothic as gothic and roman as roman, but the supposed value of this bit of pedantic nonsense escapes me. In any case, a solid block of gothic majuscules is as ugly a piece of printing as can well be imagined, and certainly not the easiest to read. If anyone should doubt this, let him puzzle over the descriptions supplied in GW 5978, 7905, or 9148. The use of several faces for bibliographical descriptions, apart from the unattractive result, seems to serve no practical purpose, particularly since, in fifteenth-century books anyway, it is not so much the *face* as the *size* of the font which is important. This information, as we have seen, should be brought out in the collational heading so that the bibliographer need only turn to this section for the precise details he may wish to have.

For those who favor reproducing gothic with gothic face, it might be well worth recalling that these reproductions of text are not always exact copies anyway. The

Gesamtkatalog possesses a truly amazing number of sorts of type in order to reproduce all the various contractions used by the fifteenth-century printer for the Latin alphabet, but in the case of Greek books these abbreviations have been silently expanded. This was, of course, necessitated by the practical impossibility of cutting anew the thirteen hundred odd sorts of type found in the Venice font of 1486.[72] Thus, while it is quite simple to supply quasi-facsimile reproductions of gothic or roman face, it is impossible to do so for Greek books. This being the case, I see no advantage in slavish copying under one set of circumstances and in liberal treatment of the problem under another. The advantages that accrue through the use of roman face for all books printed with the Latin alphabet will be self-evident to the printer of a bibliography and should present no problems to the reader of it.

So much for the modifications of the rules established by the *Gesamtkatalog*. There are further supplemental suggestions which may be worth presenting. In the textual reproductions the *Gesamtkatalog* supplies only the number of the leaf from which the extract has been taken. There are so few fifteenth-century books with correctly numbered folios, and a relatively small group where numberings can be inferred with ease, that the citation of the leaf number is usually very little help in locating the leaf in a large volume. It might be practical, therefore, to note the signature of the leaf as well, particularly when the book is signed.

The Italian *Indice* has had the happy thought of also supplying a plate to illustrate each previously unknown edition. The added expense for this feature seems trivial compared with the manifest benefit of being able to check upon the *Indice's* typographical assignment and accuracy of transcription.

Finally, the *Gesamtkatalog's* section of *Anmerkungen* can, wherever necessary, be enlarged to accommodate comments on pin-holes, watermarks, and similar bits of evidence, the evidential value of which must be left to the judgment of the individual bibliographer. The special annotations[73] will, of course, be the same as those mentioned for the incunabula already fully described.

I have spoken at some length of what I believe may represent the best form for the basic bibliographical description of incunabula. The outline, as suggested by the *Gesamtkatalog*, has been proved by those most stringent of tests, experiment and time. The modifications that I have suggested are admittedly minor.[74] They seemed desirable to me, but if they do not appear so to any other incunabulist, I shall not be bitterly aggrieved. It is not wisdom, in my opinion, to compel all scholars to employ the same set of rules. All such attempts in the past have filled the world with controversy, and it does not appear that they have brought us the desired uniformity.

Those who are interested in the most recent developments in bibliographical technique will have observed that I have not, so far, discussed two relatively new practices and suggestions. One of these, bearing the high endorsement of E. Gordon Duff,[75] deals with the position of the colophon in the textual description. Specifically, Duff suggested that whenever a fifteenth-century book contained a colophon, this should be transcribed first before proceeding to the remainder of the text as it is found in the volume. The other concerns itself with the formulary of collation and the bibliographical shorthand first set forth in practical form by Dr. W. W. Greg[76] and since amplified and extended by his admirers.[77] At the risk of appearing unprogressive, I must state that neither of these innovations appeals to me for the purpose of incunabula descriptions.

The chief argument against printing the colophon first, in close proximity to the heading, is that at best the colophon merely repeats what has already been set down in the heading, and all too rarely in such fashion that the non-expert can understand it.[78] At the very worst, putting an incorrect colophon below a correct heading can easily confuse the expert, since he has no way of knowing immediately which one is correct. The possibility is always present that the discrepancy may be the result of a simple misprint.[79]

Again, there are altogether too many colophons[80] which supply information contrary to fact[81] or contrary to modern usage.[82] The confusion, unhappily familiar to all medievalists, as to the day upon which the new year began in each city, complicated by the habits of the individual printer[83] who may have had his own ideas on the subject, can lead to relatively simple disagreements. In those instances where the printer either thoughtlessly or deliberately repeated an earlier colophon of his own[84] or one by another printer,[85] the confusion brought about by two mutually contradictory statements close together may become quite hopeless. Furthermore, it is by no means unusual to find two or more colophons in the same book,[86] each with its own date, and it occasionally happens that the preliminary matter[87] bears a date later than that found at the end of the text. What order is the bibliographer to follow and which statement is to be given preference? As I see it, there is no advantage in printing the colophon first, and the disadvantages may be considerable.[88] I should, therefore, prefer to find the colophon described in its proper place according to its position in the volume.

I have reluctantly come to the conclusion that I must be a great deal more muddle-headed than a good many of my colleagues, for the most recent exposition of the Gregian bibliographical shorthand, which it was my privilege to read in manuscript, has left me very dissatisfied.[89] The rules, devices, and practices may be perfectly simple,[90] but it seems that it will require a number of major modifications and exceptions to provide for circumstances peculiar, in large part, to fifteenth-century books. In science a rule or a formula must be universally applicable or it is useless, and, unless bibliography is willing to become not a science but a pseudo-science, this fundamental concept *must* be retained. If a satisfactory bibliographical shorthand can be set up for Elizabethan books—and I have not the slightest doubt that Dr. Greg has succeeded in doing so—that is eminently desirable; but if it does not comfortably satisfy the requirements of the incunabulist, it should not be twisted to meet these very special conditions.

I would not have any quarrel with Dr. Greg's formulary and shorthand—and could not have any—if, as he intended,[91] it were confined to STC[92] books or possibly to all books produced in the English-speaking world. But in extending it to incunabula, and thus by extension or implication to all books printed thereafter throughout Western Europe, the shorthand becomes subject to altogether too many exceptions and specific modifications to cover the existing circumstances in these books, and thus loses much of its effectiveness.

I have neither the time nor the inclination to consider every objection[93] which an incunabulist might raise against the bibliographical formulary as now set forth, but two points may be singled out for discussion. The first of these concerns the dictum that "the index should always be an even number."[94]

As I understand it,[95] the argument against permitting gatherings to be represented by uneven numbers is based on the belief that signatures should be so expressed as to reflect the methods of machining, that is, of the physical printing of the leaves. Viewed historically, of course, they do no such thing. Signatures were used in manuscripts[96] for centuries prior to the invention of printing and appear to have been borrowed by the printer from manuscript usage for the same reason they were employed by the scribe, namely, to keep the sheets in order and to insure that the binders assembled them correctly. I must here repeat what I have mentioned before, that incunabula represent the bridge between manuscripts and printed books as we know them today; they thus exhibit on occasion certain scribal practices. In this respect the special status of the earliest printed books must always be borne in mind.

It is my firm conviction, then, that manuscript and

stamped signatures,[97] as well as those occasionally found in the blocks used in the printing of block-books,[98] constitute conclusive proof that such was the historical belief as to the function of these marks. Early signatures, then, are obviously entirely independent of machining and serve no other purpose than to keep the sheets in their proper order.[99] There seems to be no particular reason to give them, in the collation, an additional meaning which they did not originally possess.

If an uneven index number for a quire is considered unsatisfactory,[100] it must be thought so because this number is regarded as reflecting either the manner of folding or that of printing. But to the binder an uneven number of leaves presents no problem since the odd leaf can be bound with the others in several different ways; such a number is thus adequate for the binder, for whose convenience signature letters and numbers were originally introduced. I hold, therefore, that the notation for the quires in the collation, as represented by their letters and numbers, should be of such sort as to indicate not the method of printing but the number of leaves which each quire ought to contain in an ideal copy. Furthermore, in my opinion, the sum total of the index numbers in the collation should always be the same as the total number of leaves in a volume. When any index numbers are uneven, an explanation is obviously required and should be provided, but I firmly believe that the best method for explaining such abnormalities is one which accords with the historical purpose of the letters and numbers of the gathering. In any case, it seems certain that the fifteenth-century printer did *not* object to

an uneven number of leaves in a quire[101] any more than
the medieval scribe did,[102] and there are numerous instances to illustrate this.

Thus the collation[103] should indicate, regardless of the
mechanical difficulties involved, the fifteenth-century
printer's intention as to the structural composition of the
book in its final form—that is, after it had passed
through the hands of the binder. That this can be done
in a perfectly simple and uncomplicated manner has
been amply demonstrated by Polain.[104] This eminent
bibliographer used uneven index numbers, but in every
instance where it was possible to do so he noted the position of the odd leaf. The reasons for the presence of
such a leaf would normally be set forth in our section of
notes and annotations. That, at least, is how I feel about
the matter.

The second major objection which must be raised
against Dr. Greg's shorthand as it now exists is the use
of π and χ.[105] If Dr. Greg had planned to make his rules
suitable for incunabula, he would certainly have been the
first to realize that his choice of arbitrary symbols was
most unhappy, since most fifteenth-century Greek books
are signed with Greek signatures![106] Among those printers[107] of the following century who employed this
method of signing may be numbered Aldus,[108] Antonio
Blado,[109] Gilles de Gourmont, [110] and Simon de
Colines.[111] For such books, π and χ, used both as arbitrary symbols and as actual signings, create an impossible
situation. This should be readily apparent to anyone who
gives it the slightest thought. If then, through this situation, the bibliographical shorthand in one of its major

contributions is not applicable to Greek books, the single, most important (culturally speaking) group of fifteenth-century books does not come within the prescribed rules. In short, it is somewhat like setting up a shorthand for Elizabethan books which cannot be made to apply to the several editions of Shakespeare's plays, numerically about the same. It would of course be comparatively simple to substitute another set of arbitrary signs, but whoever may wish to suggest new symbols should remember that there are early printed books signed in Hebrew,[112] Cyrillic,[113] Ethiopic,[114] Glagolithic,[115] Syriac,[116] and, for aught I know, other alphabets as well.

I have held forth, probably at too great length, on the topic that is the subject of this series of lectures, but there is one more observation upon which, with your indulgence, I should like to enlarge. So many people have asked me, at one time or another, *why* all this pother about incunabula. The span of little over fifty years which marks their epoch, the sceptics say, is a very short one, and these books, moreover, were produced in a period, generally speaking, of literary stagnation. No one will deny that this is quite true; there is only an occasional foreshadowing[117] of the Reformation which was so shortly thereafter, and for better or for worse, to engulf nearly the whole of the Old World. But these critics overlook one highly important truth, one which in itself accounts for many of the errors, oversights and inconsistencies in the bibliographies and catalogues I have spoken of; these should *not*, then, be criticized too severely.[118]

Though the printed books of the fifteenth century

are only in small part concerned with the contemporary literature of their day or with the problems of the decades that lay before them, the large majority of them, on the other hand, deal with the history, science, literature, and law of the previous twenty-five hundred years. They are written in, and represent the culture of, nearly all the languages of civilized Europe, west of the Vistula River and south of the Baltic Sea from the period of the Homeric poems to the age of Erasmus. And that is a very large field indeed.

NOTES

1. The earliest list of incunabula appears to have been that of 825 books belonging to the Stadtbibliothek Nürnberg and listed by J. Saubertus, *Historia bibliothecae reipublicae Noribergensis*, Noribergae, 1643.

2. Stuttgart and Paris, 1826-1838. For an account of Hain's curious life, see Erich von Rath, "Zur Biographie Ludwig Hains," *Bok-och biblioteks-historiska studier, tillägnade Isak Collijn på hans 50-årsdag*, Uppsala, 1925, pp. 161-182.

3. William Blades, *The Life and Typography of William Caxton*, London, 1861-1863; Johannes W. Holtrop, *Monuments typographiques des Pays-Bas au quinzième siècle*, La Haye, 1868; Henry Bradshaw, *A Classified Index of the Fifteenth Century Books in the de Meyer Collection at Ghent, November 1869*, London, 1870, and his *List of the Founts of Type and Woodcut Devices Used by Printers in Holland in the Fifteenth Century*, London, 1871 (both reprinted in his *Collected Papers*, Cambridge, 1889, pp. 206-236 and 258-280).

4. Robert Proctor, *An Index to the Early Printed Books in the British Museum: from the Invention of Printing to the Year MD. with Notes of those in the Bodleian Library*, London, 1898-1903.

5. Konrad Haebler, *Typenrepertorium der Wiegendrucke*, Halle a. S., 1905-1924.

6. *An Introduction to Bibliography for Literary Students*, Oxford, 1927.

7. *Catalogue of Books Printed in the XV*[th] *Century now in the British Museum*, London, 1908-1935 (referred to hereafter as BMC).

8. Leipzig, 1925-1938 (referred to hereafter as GW).

9. *Catalog Rules; Author and Title Entries*, Chicago, 1908, and Dorcas Fellows, *Cataloging Rules with Explanations and Illustrations*, New York, 1926. *The Rules for Compiling the Catalogues of*

Printed Books, Maps and Music in the British Museum, London, 1936, differ from those used in the Museum's own incunabula catalogue, nor are the Bodleian Library's *Cataloguing Rules,* [Oxford, 1939], practical for describing fifteenth-century books.

10. *The Bibliographical Society 1892-1942, Studies in Retrospect,* London, 1945, p. 27. Dr. Greg has, over a period of years, outlined his ideas as to the nature of bibliography, though his statements on occasion seem somewhat contradictory. See his "What Is Bibliography?" *Transactions of the Bibliographical Society,* XII (1911-1913), 39-53; "The Present Position of Bibliography," *Library,* 4th ser., XI (1930-1931), 241-262; "Bibliography—an Apologia," *Library,* 4th ser., XIII (1932-1933), 113-143.

11. "The Aims of Bibliography," *Library,* 4th ser., XIII (1932-1933), 225-250, together with Dr. Greg's comments (pp. 250-255) and Dr. Pollard's summary (pp. 255-257) from which the next quotation has been taken (p. 257).

12. Walter A. Copinger, "Inaugural Address," *Transactions of the Bibliographical Society,* I (1893), 34.

13. Another suitable definition is the one given by George W. Cole, "Bibliographical Problems, with a Few Solutions," *Papers of the Bibliographical Society of America* (referred to hereafter as *PBSA*), X (1915-1916), 124: "Bibliography claims as its province the consideration of all the methods by which thought is transmitted from the mind of the author to the public, but more especially the perpetuation of thought, in these latter days, by means of the printing-press." See also Victor H. Paltsits, "Bibliography, the Correct Description of Books," *Proceedings of the Second Convention of the Inter-American Bibliographical and Library Association,* Washington, D. C., 1939.

14. BMC I, ix-xxii.

15. Henry Guppy, *Rules for the Cataloguing of Incunabula,* London, 1932, a revision of his paper "Suggestions for the Cataloguing of Incunabula," *Bulletin of The John Rylands Library,* VIII (1924), 444-455. This is based in the main on BMC. In practice the *Rules* were considerably modified for the printed cata-

logue *English Incunabula in The John Rylands Library*, Manchester, 1930.

16. Arnold C. Klebs, "Desiderata in the Cataloguing of Incunabula," *PBSA*, X (1915-1916), 143-163.

17. M.-Louis Polain, *Catalogue des livres imprimés au quinzième siècle des bibliothèques de Belgique*, Bruxelles, 1932, I, v-xxi.

18. Léopold Delisle, *Instructions pour la rédaction d'un catalogue de manuscrits et pour la rédaction d'un inventaire des incunables conservés dans les bibliothèques publiques de France*, Paris [1910], pp. 49-98. It is significant for the close relationship existing between manuscripts and incunables that the rules for cataloguing both are printed in one volume. As Delisle says, in many libraries incunabula "forment une annexe des collections de manuscrits."

19. F. Madan, E. G. Duff and S. Gibson, "Standard Descriptions of Printed Books," *Oxford Bibliographical Society, Proceedings & Papers*, I (1922-1926), 55-64.

20. J. D. Cowley, *Bibliographical Description and Cataloguing*, London, 1939.

21. Arundell Esdaile, *A Student's Manual of Bibliography*, London, 1932, pp. 248-271; A. W. Pollard and W. W. Greg, "Some Points in Bibliographical Descriptions," *Transactions of the Bibliographical Society*, IX (1906-1908), 31-52, and especially F. Madan, "Degressive Bibliography," *ibid.*, 53-65; Ronald B. McKerrow, *Introduction*, pp. 145-163; George W. Cole, "The Cataloguing of Rare Books in the Henry E. Huntington Library," *Bulletin of the American Library Association*, XVI (1922), 247-257.

22. Quoted by Margaret B. Stillwell, *Incunabula and Americana*, New York, 1931, p. 29. Miss Stillwell also provides suggestions for descriptions of incunabula, pp. 19-42.

23. The GW has attempted (by implication, at least) to give the description of an "ideal" copy, listing separately variant readings when known. For fifteenth-century books in particular, it is often downright impossible to determine which is the "original" state and which is the "variant" state. For many editions, variant settings of type show no significant alteration or improvement of text. As

the BMC (I, xiv) remarks: "It is rashly assumed that the correction of misprints is a sign of a revision, and therefore of later date, both as between copy and copy and between one edition and another." But it can sometimes be shown that the reprint contains a text grossly inferior to the original. For a discussion of this point, see my paper "Variants in English Incunabula," *Bookmen's Holiday*, New York,1943, pp. 459-474. It is thus sometimes impossible to tell which setting is the original and which is the variant.

24. Isak Collijn, *Katalog der Inkunabeln der Kgl. Universitäts-Bibliothek zu Uppsala*, Uppsala and Leipzig, 1907; *Katalog der In-kunabeln der Kgl. Bibliothek in Stockholm*, Stockholm, 1914; etc.

25. Another short-title form was used by Konrad Haebler in his catalogue *Frühdrucke aus der Bücherei Victor von Klemperer*, Dresden, 1927.

26. T. M. Guarnaschelli and E. Valenziani, *Indice generale degli incunaboli delle biblioteche d'Italia*, [Rome], 1943.

27. A detail which is often omitted but should be included is the measurement of the type-page since it can be used to show the size of the volume at the time it left the printer's hands. Cf. my paper "The Margins in Mediaeval Books," *PBSA*, XL (1946), 32-42.

28. "Thus bibliography and textual criticism appear to interlock in a manner that makes it difficult if not impossible to separate their respective fields and leads one to wonder whether it may not in the end be necessary to bring most textual criticism within the province of bibliography," Greg, *Studies*, p. 30.

29. Margaret B. Stillwell, *Incunabula in American Libraries, a Second Census . . .* , New York, 1940 (referred to hereafter as *Second Census*), no. A858.

30. Marie Pellechet [and M.-Louis Polain], *Catalogue général des incunables des bibliothèques publiques de France*, Paris, 1897-1909, no. 1175.

31. Panzer I: 240, 476; Maittaire I:698; Hain 4989; Voulliéme-Köln 324; Pell 3566; Polain 1065; BMC I:299; GW 6688; Morgan-Bennett 115; Schreiber 3753; Brunet I:1886; Graesse

II:139; Muther 413; Borchling-Claussen 312; Kronenberg-Deventer 95; Hawkins 82; Mazarine 1078; *Bibliotheca Spenceriana,* III:281-7; Museum Meermanno-Westreenianum II: 562; Schramm VIII:12; John Carter Brown 32; Bohatta-Liechtenstein 277 (and others cited there); Hind I:207 and II:362; etc.

32. Such as is given, for example, for the first edition of Sebastian Brant's *Das Narrenschiff,* Basel, Bergmann, 11 February 1494. See GW, IV, cols. 671-678, though it is obvious that this work still requires bibliographical examination of a technical nature along the lines of Greg's exemplary study *The Variants in the First Quarto of "King Lear,"* London, 1940.

33. *Medieval Texts and their First Appearance in Print,* London, 1943.

34. For example, GW (VII, col. 213) intimates that it will enter the *Court of Sapience (Curia Sapientiae)* under Lydgate, who certainly had nothing to do with it; cf. edition by Robert Spindler, Leipzig, 1927, pp. 80-105. GW 8385-8394 are not Italian translations of the *Vitae et sententiae philosophorum* by Diogenes Laertius; see my note in *Speculum,* XII (1937), 451-452. The GW (VI, col. 420) states that it will enter the *Chapelet des vertus* under Laurent (Frère) who was certainly not the author of this work; on this, compare my article in the *Publications of the Modern Language Association,* LXII (1947), 32-44. The *Dicta philosophorum* is the heading for this work although the authors and the literary history of this work are well-known (*Early English Text Society, Original Series,* no. 211, pp. ix-xiii).

35. The eminent astronomer, Johann Müller of Koenigsberg, is listed under Müller (BMC), Johannes Regiomontanus (GW, according to the *Second Census,* p. 427) and Regiomontanus, Johannes (*Second Census*). Similarly the important *Calendrier des bergers* (GW 5906-5914) is hidden away under the heading "Ephemerides" both in the Museum's general catalogue (cf. new edition, XXX, 782) and in [Sir] Henry Thomas, *Short-title Catalogue of Books Printed in France and of French Books Printed in other Countries from 1470 to 1600, now in the British Museum,* London, 1924,

pp. 151-152. The Kommission für den Gesamtkatalog der Wiegendrucke itself varies its practice; in the *Einblattdrucke des XV. Jahrhunderts*, Halle, 1914, the entry is Engel, Johannes (nos. 546-552; twice the Christian name is Johann) though the same writer is called Angeli, Johannes in GW 1892-1904. For other examples, see notes 36 and 69.

36. *Imitatio Christi*, for example, is the heading in BMC, though the old BM general catalogue lists the work under Charlier de Gerson, Jean, and in the new edition it will appear under Jesus Christ. The Bibliothèque Nationale entry, by the way, is Gerson, Jean Charlier de Gerson. In BMC, *Belial* is assigned to Jacobus (Palladinus) de Theramo; the author in the general catalogue is Palladinus, Jacobus, while Palladini (Giacomo) is the form in the index to the catalogue of the BM's Royal and Kings MSS (for MS. 6 E III, the heading is Iacobus de Theramo). In the description of Harley MS. 51, the author is Theramo, Jacobus de, while the work is entitled *Peccatorum consolatio*. The *Meditationes vitae Christi* is listed under Bonaventura in BMC, under Bonaventura "doubtful and supposititious works" in the new general catalogue, and as "perhaps by Johannes de Caulibus" in the case of Royal MS. 8 B I. See also the next note.

37. The *Copulata tractatuum* by Petrus Hispanus (the listing is John XXI, Pope, in the British Museum's old general catalogue) is to be found under three slightly varying titles in the first volume of BMC (pp. 198, 274 and 297). So also the *Confessionale* by St. Antoninus is entitled "De instructione" (I:32), "Confessionale" (I:90) and "Summa confessionum" (I:181). Aegidius Suchtelensis is cited (BMC I:272) as the author of a work listed anonymously under "Elegantiae" (III:629) and under "Elegantiarum viginti praecepta" (III:650). A curious instance is the *Expositio mysteriorum missae* (GW 3222 and 3224) which is entered under "Expositio" (III:651) and under Balthasar, Frater (III:627). The former edition was listed under Liturgies (col. 232) and the latter under Jesus Christ (col. 121) in the old general catalogue, though both appear under Balthasar in the new (IX, 750). The *Vita S. Rochi* is ascribed to Franciscus Diedus (Francesco Diedo of the general cata-

logue) in BMC VI:710 and 760, but to Maldura, Petrus Ludovicus, in I:49 (for explanation, see GW 8331).

38. In certain cases it seems preferable to use the mediaeval form rather than the one presently conjectured to be the "correct" one; cf. my review of Goldschmidt's book, *PBSA*, XXXVII (1943), 310-314.

39. Dr. Greg has repeatedly urged that "bibliography has nothing to do with the subject-matter of books" (*Library*, 4th ser., XIII (1932-1933), 114). In the same essay he made an amusing suggestion: "Nobody would think of editing a text that had no meaning, and nobody would choose to edit a text in a language he did not understand—though it might be a very interesting exercise." I could certainly agree with Greg if his statement were confined to the comparative textual value (esthetically or otherwise) of different texts or variants. But the subject-matter itself, as in the case cited above, can be valuable bibliographical evidence.

Again the text can sometimes provide information not otherwise ascertainable. The only fifteenth-century edition of the *De astrologica veritate* by Lucius Bellantius is dated in all the bibliographies (e.g., GW 3802) as having been printed 9 May 1498 by Gerardus de Harlem in Florence. In the text (sign. s5 recto), however, we find Bellantius' boast which may be freely translated to the effect that there were "very many Florentine witnesses worthy of belief to whom I predicted by observing Savonarola's ruling-constellation five months before his overthrow, while he was still flourishing, both that Savonarola would incline to heresy and that he would end his life at the noose." Savonarola, of course, was first hanged and then burnt on Wednesday, 23 May 1498 (Joseph Schnitzer, *Savonarola, ein Kulturbild aus der Zeit der Renaissance*, München, 1924, I, 579-584). It is thus certain that the book was printed after the date as given in the colophon.

40. See note 34.

41. Dietrich Reichling, *Appendices ad Hainii-Copingeri Repertorium bibliographicum*, München, 1905-1914.

42. Except for the first which contains an explanatory heading.

For liturgical incunabula, it was common practice for the printer to add letters indicating the local "use" to the signature. In his 1517 Aristides, F. Giunta printed "Arist." in the signature line of every quire beginning with signature "g".

43. It is pertinent to note that Francisci (or Antonio di Francesco) was a Venetian (compare also BMC VI:xvii) and this may account for the dialectal form.

44. Compare BMC VI:671 (IA 27723).

45. For a summary of such possible practice, see Edwin Wolf 2nd, "Press Corrections in Sixteenth- and Seventeenth-Century Quartos," *PBSA*, XXXVI (1942), 187-198, and Francis R. Johnson, "Press Corrections and Presswork in the Elizabethan Printing Shop," *PBSA*, XL (1946), 276-286. Mr. Johnson doubts that this method was ever used but, since it is mechanically quite possible, it should—in theory anyway—not be dismissed lightly. See also Appendix I.

46. *Catalogue of Manuscripts and Early Printed Books . . . now forming Portion of the Library of J. Pierpont Morgan*, London, 1907, III, 3-33, and my paper "Three *Horae ad Usum Sarum* Printed by Philippe Pigouchet," *Library*, 4th ser., XIX (1938-1939), 304-310.

47. For a fuller account, compare *Gutenberg-Jahrbuch*, 1936, pp. 68-72. The first printed appearance of the text was in the German version.

48. Walter A. Copinger, *Supplement to Hain's Repertorium bibliographicum*, London, 1895-1902.

49. By repetition there are 118 cuts; for further details, see my paper, *loc. cit.*

50. Konrad Haebler, *Bibliografía Ibérica del siglo XV*, La Haya, 1903-1917.

51. Ada Thurston and Curt F. Bühler, *Check List of Fifteenth Century Printing in The Pierpont Morgan Library*, New York, 1939, no. 1749.

52. Martin Kurz, *Handbuch der iberischen Bilderdrucke des XV.*

Jahrhunderts, Leipzig, 1931, no. 217. The heading there is Johannes de Capua, *Directorium humanae vitae* (in Spanish). Kurz notes that the only known copy (in Madrid BN) is both incomplete and misbound which may account for the omissions and differing order in his listing.

53. Arnold C. Klebs, *Incunabula scientifica et medica*, Bruges, 1938, nos. 344.1-2 and 345.1-7.

54. Compare Sir John E. Sandys, *A History of Classical Scholarship*, Cambridge, 1903-1908, III, 127-131.

55. This is a fuller account of the discussion first printed in vol. I.

56. This may indeed lead to serious confusion. For example, in Weale-Bohatta's *Catalogus Missalium* (London, 1928, no. 811), a Regensburg *Missal* is dated "1500, XV. kal. Jan. (15 Dec.)." This is, of course, an impossible resolution and one might conjecture that the printed date was "XV. kal. Jan." (i.e., December 18th). Actually the date in the book is "XVIII. kal. Jan." and December 15th is the correct reading.

57. This does not necessarily follow, for by cutting in half the "carta regalis" and the "carta communis" and printing with half-sheets, the printer could attain quartos the size of folios and octavos of the dimensions of the usual quarto. This is proved by the many cases where quarto sheets are intermixed with folios and octavos with quartos; for further discussion of this point, see Konrad Haebler, *Handbuch der Inkunabelkunde*, Leipzig, 1925, p. 40.

58. GW 4205, GW 4206 and GW 4208.

59. GW 4229, GW 4230 and GW 4235.

60. And then only when a bibliographer copied verbatim another's description without examining the original. Fortunately this rather haphazard method is falling into disfavor.

61. See his catalogues cited in note 24.

62. The confusion that may result from not properly identifying the blank leaves in a volume is amply demonstrated in my note "The First Edition of Ausonius," *PBSA*, XLI (1947), 60. See also note 100.

63. For example: Hamann (GW 5111, 5164); Arrivabene (GW 5118); Renner (GW 4223, 5103, 6129); Torresanus (GW 5113, 5115); Koberger (GW 5219); Amerbach (GW 4248); Meister and Kollicker (*Gutenberg-Jahrbuch*, 1927, p. 9); Caxton (Duff, *Fifteenth Century English Books*, Oxford, 1917, nos. 164 and 172). So also in the sixteenth century, Blado (Chantilly 721) and the Giuntas (Church Americana catalogue 99).

64. See his catalogues of the Western manuscripts in the Cambridge libraries: Trinity College (1900-1904), Gonville and Caius (1907), St. John's (1913), Pepys (1923), etc.

65. *Catalogue raisonné des premières impressions de Mayence*, Mainz, 1911. Cowley (*op. cit.*, p. 95) also recommends the use of arabic numbers. Polain does not inclose the inferred quire numerals in brackets; there is, thus, no distinction made between actual signings with arabic numbers (as in the case of Polain 869) and those that have been inferred (Polain 902).

66. Compare, for example, the first five editions of the *De civitate Dei* by St. Augustine as collated by the GW (nos. 2874-2878) and by BMC (IV:2, 5, 10, 24 and V:153). The collation for Cicero's *De natura deorum* etc., [Venice], Vindelinus de Spira, 1471, differs in many places between GW 6902 and BMC V:158.

67. Ernst Consentius, "Die Typen und der Gesamtkatalog der Wiegendrucke," *Gutenberg Jahrbuch*, 1932, pp. 55-109, and the reply by Carl Wehmer, "Zur Beurteilung des Methodenstreits in der Inkunabelkunde," *Gutenberg Jahrbuch*, 1933, pp. 250-325. For the problems concerning the identification and classification of roman types, see Lester Condit, *A Provisional Index to Roman Printing Types of the 15th Century*, Chicago, 1935. The question as it affects the following century has been discussed by A. F. Johnson, "The Supply of Types in the Sixteenth Century," *Library*, 4th ser., XXIV (1943-1944), 47-65.

68. See BMC II:387—IB 6740, where the note reads: "Types: 180, Canon; 130, large text in the chants and small in the Canon; 112, small text in the chants, large text elsewhere; 104, foliation;

92 (leaded), small text, and notice on 9ᵃ." Cf. also BMC VI:768 and 827.

69. Haebler, *Bibliografía Ibérica*, lists the work as *Compendio de la salud humana*, Saragossa, Hurus, 15 August 1494; actually this is a Spanish translation of the well-known *Fasciculus medicinae* by Johannes de Ketham (Klebs 575.1).

70. So GW, Collijn, Leiv Amundsen (*Katalog over Universitetsbibliotekets paleotypsamling*, Oslo, 1926), and Borchling-Claussen (*Niederdeutsche Bibliographie*, Neumünster, 1931-1936) but not Reichling, Haebler (*Bibliografía Ibérica*), Jörgen Bölling (*Index librorum saeculo XVᵐᵒ impressorum quorum exempla possidet Bibliotheca Regia Hafniensis*, Hafniae, 1889-1898), or Nijhoff-Kronenberg (*Nederlandsche bibliographie van 1500 tot 1540*, 's-Gravenhage, 1923-1940).

71. For example BMC, Duff, Guppy, as well as Pellechet and Polain among Continental incunabulists.

72. Robert Proctor, *The Printing of Greek in the Fifteenth Century*, Oxford, 1900, p. 75: "Thus the number of sorts may be, I think, safely put down as not much, if at all, less than 1350."

73. I should also like to urge that more attention be paid to the manuscript notes and additions found in many incunabula—and that items of literary interest be at least itemized in the catalogues of incunabula. Strict bibliographers will claim that manuscript notes are not their concern, and this is, no doubt, quite true. But unless the bibliographer or cataloguer does study these oddments, who is there to do this very necessary job? It would obviously be absurd to divide the responsibility for the description of a composite volume and to refer the manuscript passages (often confined to a few pages) to the department of manuscripts. That many items of literary and historical interest lie hidden away in the uncatalogued manuscript sections of fifteenth-century *Sammelbände* is common knowledge, and it is certainly the duty of those to whose care the incunabula are committed to make these tracts available. What such studies can bring to light is shown by Dr. Dorothy M. Schullian's article "Old Volumes Shake Their Vellum Heads," *Bulletin of the Medical*

Library Association, XXXIII (1945), 413-448; compare also *Traditio*, IV (1946), 429-435, for my series "Libri impressi cum notis manuscriptis."

74. For a sample description in accordance with these suggestions, see Appendix I.

75. *Oxford Bibliographical Society Proceedings & Papers*, I (1922-1926), 56 and 60. This method had been previously recommended by Falconer Madan, "Degressive Bibliography," as previously cited, pp. 54 and 64.

76. "A Formulary of Collation," *Library*, 4th ser., XIV (1933-1934), 365-382, and applied in his *A Bibliography of the English Printed Drama to the Restoration*, London, 1939. Much of this is an extension of the suggestions set forth by McKerrow in his *Introduction to Bibliography*, pp. 155-163.

77. See the forthcoming book on "Principles of Descriptive Bibliography" by Professor Fredson T. Bowers.

78. See for example BMC I:133 (IB 1831): "imp̄ss⁹ ē Argētine. Anno dñi. M.cccc.lxxxv. & finit⁹ in die sācto♃ marti♃"; BMC VI:741 (IC 26345): "Imp̄ssuʒ Ml'i per Beninuʒ & Ioanneʒ antoniū de honate"; or BMC VII:1084 (IA 34103): "Explicit br̄uiariū ſʒ curiā Romanā. Imp̄ssū Nonātule duc³. Mutīe p̲ nos Georgiū & Antoniū frēs d'mischmīs ciues mut³."

79. Thus (*Second Census* G632) "xxxiiij Kal. Oct.", (BMC VII:1015) "33 March 1495," and (GW 7548) "8 Nov. 1493" [for 1494] might not be recognized as errors in the originals but understood as slips on the part of the bibliographer. Cf. also *Second Census* G1 and G2.

80. The BMC (I:x) estimated that perhaps 45 per cent of the fifteenth-century editions were unsigned, an estimate borne out by the studies of Carl Wehmer (*Gutenberg Jahrbuch*, 1933, 267-271) and of E. von Kathen ("Statistisches zu GW VI und VII. 1," *Beiträge zur Inkunabelkunde, neue folge*, I (1935), 112-113). For nearly half the books, then, there is no colophon to be transcribed first and thus there would be some lack of uniformity in the descriptions if this method were adopted.

81. Typographical examination, for example, shows that an edition of the *Fiore di virtù* which (the colophon declares) was printed at Venice, Nel Beretin Convento, 1477, was certainly produced by the Ripoli Press in Florence (BMC VI:621). Again, one of the two editions of the *Regimen sanitatis Salernitanum* claiming to have been printed in Strassburg, 29 December 1491, was actually printed in Venice by Bernardinus Benalius (BMC V:379). For the books by Pachel and Scinzenzeler with a Venetian imprint, consult BMC VI:xxvi-xxvii. Then there are colophons which have been proved incorrect by documentary evidence; see the Ptolemy (BMC VI:814) and the Xenophon (BMC VI:734 and xxv). For the *Psalterio in volgare* of 1476, still other criteria prove its Milanese rather than Venetian origin (BMC VI:xxiv and 733). See also Alfred W. Pollard, *An Essay on Colophons*, Chicago, 1905, pp. 46-47, for accidental misdatings.

82. For example, the many German books with obscure or difficult liturgical dates printed at Augsburg by Sorg, Bämler, and Schönsperger.

83. Compare Richard C. Christie, "The Chronology of the Early Aldines," *Bibliographica*, I (1895), 193-222, and BMC V:lii. See Pollard, *ibid.*, pp. 170-184.

84. In many cases the colophons were repeated verbatim; thus GW 7639 is an exact copy of GW 7638 and GW 8217 of GW 8216. Occasionally the wording and arrangement will differ, though the information conveyed by the colophons is the same; cf. Duff 124 vs. Duff 123a and GW 7594 vs. GW 7591. Compare also Pollard, *op. cit.*, pp. 159-169.

85. See *Second Census* G62, P487, P580, P587, S559, etc.

86. Three and four colophons are quite common (GW 9073-9076 and 9149-9159). There are seven in Hain 11768 (BMC V:366) and eight in Hain 11767 (BMC VII:1001).

87. For prefaces dated later than colophons, see *Epistolae Graecae* (BMC V:560), Homer (BMC VI:678) and Crastonus (BMC VII:1067). For supplementary material with a later date, compare the Lascaris (BMC V:552).

88. McKerrow, *Transactions of the Bibliographical Society*, XII (1911-1913), 282: "We sometimes find a *colophon* containing a date reprinted from an earlier edition without change. This is perhaps due to simple carelessness. For this reason dates in colophons should be regarded as of little weight, if other evidence tends to show that they are incorrect."

89. I should here like to express my deep gratitude to Professor Fredson T. Bowers. Although we do not agree on many main issues, my task in setting forth my own ideas as to the form bibliographical descriptions should take has been materially aided by the exposition of his own views. His kindness in making his notes readily available to me is an example of scholarly coöperation all too rarely encountered. It is to be understood, of course, that he is in no way responsible for any conclusions (or possible errors) as set forth above.

90. There is always a danger in using any form of shorthand in that succeeding generations may not be able to understand it readily. Hain, for example, developed a very abbreviated form, and there may be many bibliographers who might have difficulty with such a summary as occurs in Hain 7279: "s. l. a. et typ. n. 4. g. ch. c.ſ. et ff. n. 39 et 40 l. 232 ff. num. (num. 203 defic.) et 10 ff. non num." Naturally there are many suggestions by Greg which can be suitably adopted for incunables, such as 5A rather than AAAAA and the use of a superior number where the same letters are repeated a number of times in a (regularly printed) book. But see Appendix II.

91. Greg (*Library*, 4th ser., XIV (1933-1934), 382) states: "This, so far as my experience goes, provides for all the more unusual abnormalities in the make-up of English books of the sixteenth and seventeenth centuries."

92. A. W. Pollard and G. R. Redgrave, *A Short-title Catalogue of Books Printed in England, Scotland, & Ireland and of English Books Printed Abroad, 1475-1640*, London, 1926.

93. For further details, see Appendix II.

94. Greg (*ibid.*, p. 378) says: "It follows that (in my opinion) the index should always be an even number." McKerrow, as the note on the same page explains, did not agree with Greg; cf. his

Introduction, pp. 160-161 and 194-195. One of the finest catalogues of recent years (*The Carl H. Pforzheimer Library*, *English Literature, 1475-1700*, New York, 1940) is not averse to using uneven index numbers.

95. This implication is drawn from the several statements made by Dr. Greg on pp. 378-379, largely to the effect that the index numbers should "indicate the make-up as well" and that "every quire, as printed, consisted of an even number of leaves, and we may therefore indicate its make-up by an even index number." In my view, however, the signatures (as printed in the incunable and as stated in the collation) simply represent the printer's intention without reference to folding, imposition or other physical operation. Thus the *letter* indicates the position of the *quire* in relation to the other quires, and the *number* the position of the *sheet* (or leaf) in respect to the others in that quire. In any event, for the (unfortunately too many) editions known only from fragments or incomplete copies, it is clearly quite often impossible to write a collation which in any way expresses the original make-up. For such volumes, the collation can at best show only what is presently preserved. In the case of early books containing single-page printing, the formulary would correctly show the folding but certainly not the method of printing.

96. Signatures are to be found in the Codex Sinaiticus of the fourth century (cf. the facsimile edition by Kirsopp Lake, Oxford, 1921-1922, I, xvi, and II, xix). The earliest manuscript with signatures in the Pierpont Morgan Library appears to be the ninth-century Bede, *Explanationes in Samuelem* (MS 335). For further notes on the early use of signatures in manuscripts, see Edward K. Rand, *A Survey of the Manuscripts of Tours*, Cambridge (Mass.), 1929, I, 18-23, and Sir Edward Maunde Thompson, *An Introduction to Greek and Latin Palaeography*, Oxford, 1912, pp. 53-54.

97. For manuscript and stamped signatures, compare Haebler, *Inkunabelkunde*, pp. 50-51. I am obliged to the kindness of Mr. Philip Robinson in drawing my attention to the curious manuscript signatures in the Phillipps copy of Caxton's *Recuyell of the Hystoryes*

of Troye, [Bruges, 1475]. A characteristic quire of ten leaves is not signed R-R5 but R, R1, R2, R3, and R4 (the last being equal to the usual R5). Such signatures in manuscript (particularly when, as in this case, only part of the manuscript signings are preserved) cannot be used in the collational heading and the book must be treated as unsigned, though they may be used with caution in referring to the leaves. It seems to me optional whether stamped signatures are admitted into the collation or not.

98. See Wilhelm L. Schreiber, *Manuel de l'amateur de la gravure sur bois et sur métal au XVe siècle*, Leipzig and Berlin, 1891-1911, IV—"Biblia pauperum" (p. 3 ff.), "Apocalypsis Johannis" (p. 163 ff.), "Ars moriendi" (p. 258 ff.), etc.

99. Haebler (*loc. cit.*) says: "Einem ähnlichen Zwecke, wie das Registrum haben die Signaturen gedient, und diese sind im Gegensatz zu jenem zweifellos eine deutsche Erfindung. Der Gebrauch der Signaturen ist vermutlich fast ebenso alt, wie die Druckkunst selbst. Es ist ganz einleuchtend, dass es eines bequemen Hilfsmittels bedurfte, um aus den Haufen roher Druckbogen die Hunderte von Exemplaren eines und desselben Buches zusammenzustellen."

100. If I understand the formulary correctly, the procedure for an uneven folio quire would be something like this. When a printer produced a nine-leaf quire, the formulary might, for example, read $\$^{10}$ ($-\$9$). Now this would indicate that the ninth leaf had been deleted, perhaps because it was a blank and thus interrupted the text. If a copy subsequently came to light with the blank leaf (possibly accidentally and erroneously) preserved, the formulary might have to be revised to read $\$^{10}$ without immediate notification to the effect that the leaf was redundant and should have been deleted. In a sense, then, the formulary might no longer be describing an "ideal" copy, though it would certainly be describing a complete one. On the other hand, one would be faced by an even greater difficulty (as I see it) if the above quire had been originally described by the formulary as $\$^{8}$ ($\$1 + 1$). If a copy with the blank then turned up, how could this be noted in the collation without considerable difficulty?

I should prefer to list this quire as "$\$^{9}$($\$2$ disjunct)" or

"$ß^9$(5 + 4, 2nd leaf inserted)." If a copy with the blank leaf then turned up, I should be inclined to keep the old notation with a statement "blank conjugate of $ß2$ present in—"; possibly "$ß^9$ (blank conjugate of $ß2$ preserved in—)" might do. On the other hand, if the blank leaf does not separate two leaves of continuous text but is found at the beginning or at the end of a part of text (where a natural break occurs), I feel the bibliographer is justified in assuming that the leaf would have been deliberately preserved by the printer and thus forms an integral part of the book.

An excellent example of this problem is furnished by Mombritius, *Sanctuarium*, [Milan, *ca.* 1477]—Hain 11544, BMC VI:736. The curious arrangement of the signatures is explained by the fact that the letters depend on the names of the saints whose lives form the subject matter of the book; thus all saints whose names begin with A are found in quires "a—viii a." In order to complete the lives of the C Saints, the printer needed exactly seven leaves for the last such quire "viiii c"; the next quire "d" begins the life of St. Datius, Bishop of Milan (d. 552). In order to accomplish this, the printer set up his copy in the following manner. The first sheet is unsigned (and the first half of this is blank), the second is signed "viiii ci," the third "viiii cii," and the fourth "viiii ciii." Now the blank leaf is cut away in many copies (BMC, Brussels *Boll.*, BPubL, NewL and LCH) but is preserved in PML, HarvCL, HEHL (misbound) and Paris *BSGenev*. Are we to presume that the "ideal" copy contains "$9c^8$"? But in that case the blank leaf interrupts the text, and the leaf signed "viiii ci" becomes, according to the formulary reference, "$9c2$('viiii ci')". I think it might be simpler to describe this quire as "viiii c^7 (c7 disjunct; blank conjugate present in PML etc.)." Of course, the same situation prevails in quire "a" where the first leaf is blank and the actual text begins on "a1" [a2('a1') of the formulary], but in this case I would consider the blank leaf as being intentionally present as well as the blank last leaves "dddd8" and "gggg8." But the problem posed by blank leaves is very difficult; frankly, no completely satisfactory solution has presented itself to me.

101. The proof for this seems to me self-evident. In the first edition, of course, an uneven number of leaves in a quire may be

accounted for in a variety of ways. But when in subsequent reprints of the same book the printer continued to have uneven numbers of leaves in a quire, it is clear that he was not at all averse to this practice. For example, Polain 3314 was set up from Polain 3313 but both have 11 leaves in quire [63] (5 + 6, le 11ᵉ encarté); also Polain 1678 and 1681 were set up from 1677, but all have 9 leaves in quire "mm" (4 + 5, le 8ᵉ encarté). Particularly significant for this argument are Polain 2458/9. Both have 9 leaves in the fifth quire *but* 2458 has (4 + 5, le 8ᵉ encarté) while 2459 has (5 + 4, le 5ᵉ encarté). Clearly for the second edition (whichever one that may have been) the printer planned to have the same number of uneven leaves as in the earlier edition of this particular quire, though the actual machining differed.

102. See the descriptions of Royal MSS. 15 C X, 15 D VI, 17 C XXXIII, etc., and the comments by Rand, *op. cit.*, I, 18. For the curious composition of BM Addit. 34193, compare my *Dicts* (Early English Text Society, Original Series, No. 211, pp. xxvi-xxvii).

103. This opinion is also expressed by McKerrow (*Introduction*, p. 158, n. 1): "Collations are intended to represent the bound, or finished, book, not the sheets as they came from the press."

104. For examples, see note 101 above.

105. The use of π and χ had been previously suggested by McKerrow and Greg (*Introduction*, pp. 156 and 162).

106. Rather rarely (fortunately) one finds Greek signatures for special quires in non-Greek books, e.g., the Basel, 1533, edition of Peter Martyr (George W. Cole, *A Catalogue of Books Relating to the Discovery and Early History of North and South America forming a Part of the Library of E. D. Church*, New York, 1907, I, 151).

107. Other printers of the sixteenth century to use Greek signatures include: Johann Bebel (Basel); Zacharias Callierges and Angelus Collotius (Rome); Sebastian Greyff (Lyons); Pierre Gaudoul, Pierre Gromors and Conrad Neobar (Paris); Thierry Martens (Louvain); Bartolomeo Zanetti and Fratres de Sabio (Venice); etc.

108. So also his successors, Andreas Torresanus (Lucian, 1522) and Federicus Torresanus (*Etymologicum Graecum*, 1549).

109. Theophylactus, Rome, 1542 (PML 248—*Catalogue of a Collection of Books formed by James Toovey . . . the Property of J. Pierpont Morgan*, New York, 1901, p. 182).

110. Homer, *Batrachomyomachia*, Paris, 1507 (Proctor, *The Printing of Greek in the Fifteenth Century*, Oxford, 1900, pp. 142 and 205).

111. Sophocles, Paris, 1528 (Ph. Renouard, *Bibliographie des éditions de Simon de Colines 1520-1546*, Paris, 1894, p. 128).

112. See the two earliest Hebrew Bibles (GW 4198 and 4199), Moses ben Nachman (Lisbon, 1489—Morgan *Check List* 1850), etc.

113. For example, the Gospels printed at Braşov, 1560-1561; compare Mario Roques, "L'Évangéliaire Roumain de Coresi," *Romania*, XXXVI (1907), 429-434. There are many early books printed in and signed with "Tserkovni" (Church Slavonic) characters; cf. T. H. Darlow and H. F. Moule, *Historical Catalogue of the Printed Editions of Holy Scripture*, London, 1903-1911, IV, 1398 ff. Such signatures were also used in the Oktōēkhos printed near Cetinje in 1493/4 (Proctor 9841; BM general catalogue "Liturgies," col. 30; *Serapeum*, IV (1843), 326-327).

114. Thus the Ethiopic *Psalter*, Rome, 1513 (PML 34177).

115. See the *Breviarium Romanum* (in Croatian), Venice, 1493 (GW 5171) and Michael de Carcano, *Confessionale* (in Croatian), Zengg, 1496 (GW 6127—Verbesserung).

116. So the New Testament in Syriac, Vienna, 1556 (PML 23195).

117. In the words of Victor Scholderer (BMC VII:xxxvii): "Thus the books published in Italy, say, in 1480 do not greatly differ in kind from those still in demand twenty years later, and an account which consists of little more than statistics is often adequate within a particular group. The contribution of the North to early printing is in many respects inferior to that of Italy, but it has at any rate this interest that it shows the Northern mind here and there definitely on the move; as Dr. Pollard has noted in the case of Germany, the book-trade of that country perceptibly reflects the increasing preoccupation of thoughtful men with new ideas in reli-

gion and points the way to the coming of the Reformation within a few decades. Whatever the qualities of the Italian incunabula, we cannot find in them any prefigurement of a new outlook on life."

118. No one, I trust, will think that I have singled out the British Museum's catalogue of fifteenth-century books for unwarranted criticism, for this would be quite untrue. It just happens that BMC, being so excellent a catalogue, has many examples of every sort to offer the reader. In view of the scope and detail of this work, the occasional slight errors and lapses are relatively inconsequential. In common with other laborers in this field, I am happy to admit the heavy debt I owe to BMC.

Appendix I

As a sample for the form incunabula descriptions should take according to the provisions set forth above, we may consider a book recently acquired by the Pierpont Morgan Library (PML 38939). Although previously described by Reichling, his account contains a sufficient number of errors and omissions to warrant a new description *in toto*. Reichling described this book while it was misbound; he misread the name of the author and failed to include an analysis of the types; and there are other additions and corrections to be supplied. This is the description:

Ramírez de Villaescusa de Haro, Diego. 1459-1537. (Dean of Jaen and Granada, then successively Bishop of Astorga, Malaga and Cuenca; variously Ambassador to Flanders, France and England.)

Dialogi quattuor super auspicato Hispaniarum principis emortuali die [with salutation by Gaspar Armengotus]. Antwerp: Govaert Bac, 12 July 1498.

Reichling 1892.

4°. 40 leaves. a-e⁸. 32-38 lines. Type-page(f. 5, 37 lines): 152x88 mm. (with marginalia 108 mm.). Types: 1:99G (title and headings on b2, b4 and e7ᵛ), 2:180G (first line of title), 3:82G with M in both states (text). Guide-letters. Rubric:α,β. 4 woodcuts (by repetition, 6).

f. 1 (title): Dialogi quattuor super ‖ auspicato Hispania ♃ p'ncipis emortuali die Ja-‖cobo á villascusa auctore q̃ʒ celeberrimo nouissi-‖me impressi foeliciter incipiũtur ‖ [woodcut] ‖ ¶ Foelix quem faciũt aliena pericula cautũ ‖ Est fortunatus foelix diuesqʒ beatus ‖ 1ᵛ: ¶ Gaspar armengotus morem gerendi cupidissimus cōspicu‖um Virū Jacobū Ramireʒ Hispalensem decanum ͵pmeritum ‖ Plrurima salute impartiri iubet. ‖ Tametsi Littera ♃ monumētis ͵ppemodum innumera ͵pdita ‖ fuere cōspicue vir: . . . (ends 2 - a2, 1. 28): . . . Vale in ‖ [letters wanting]num. § § § .∴ ‖ 2ᵛ. Inuictissimae isabelae hispaniaruʒ & siciliae augustae clarissi-‖mae & saeuae mort7: de obitu ioānis serenissimi eiusdē filij vnici: ‖ iacobo á villascusa in theologia ͵pfessore īitiato: gienensi d'cano: ‖ illustrissimae ioannae archiducis austriae ͵ptosacerdote aucto-‖re: dialogus. ‖ [woodcut] ‖ 3 - a3: ¶ Mors ‖ (v³)bi nā est ioānes vidistis ne illū ? . . . 9 - b1: rium esse. Vt cum dicitʳ: si deus hoc sciuit futuruʒ: erit: ita expo-‖. . . (ends 9ᵛ - b1ᵛ, 1. 10): . . . Salmāticae .iiij. nonas octobres Anno christianae salu‖tis. M.cccc.xcvij. ‖ 10 - b2: ¶ Serenissimi atqʒ inuictissimi Fernandi hispa‖nia♃ & siciliae reg7 de obitu inclyti ioānis charis-‖simi filij illustrissimaeqʒ margaritae ei9 dulcissi-‖mae nurus dialogus consolatorius ‖ [woodcut] ‖ 10ᵛ: ¶ Ferdinandus ‖ (s⁴)Alue illustrissima filia. . . . (ends 11ᵛ - b3ᵛ, 1. 36): . . . ¶ M. Vale tu q̊ʒ pientissime parens ‖ 12 - b4: ¶ Fernandi quinti & isabelae hispaniarū & sicili-‖ae regis & reginae clarissimo♃ inuictissimorūqʒ ‖ de obitu ioannis eo♃ charissimi gnati dialogus ‖ consolatorius ‖ [woodcut] ‖ 12ᵛ: ¶ Ferdinandus ‖ (s³)Salue reginarum oīm decus. . . . (ends 39 - e7, 1. 34): . . . ibiqʒ q̄ʒ-‖tum ex alto dabitʳ: flentem maesti consolabimur. ‖ 39ᵛ: ¶ Fernand9 rex. Isabela regina Margarita vi‖dua colloquuntur. ‖ [woodcut] ‖ ¶ Fer Salue margarita filia su͟p ōnes mihi chara ‖ . . . (ends 40 - e8, 1. 37): . . . īfoelicis infaustiqʒ obit9 vulnera ‖ refricentur. ‖ 40ᵛ (colophon): ¶ Impressum hantwerpiae p̱ me Godfridū back. ‖ Anno ab incarnatiōe. M.cccc. octauo et ‖ nonagesimo Die v'o. xij. mēſʒ ‖ Julij. F I N I S ‖ [woodcut] ‖

Signatures appear on the first and third leaves of each quire, except al [*or* Signatures on ₰1,3(-al) only]. Folio 22 (c6) contains but 29 lines of text, followed by the rhyming note:

> ¶ Qua*m*uis spaciu*m* detur
> t*ame*n null*us* defectus habe*tur*.

The woodcuts are: (1) a King (Ferdinand) and a young lady (Princess Margaret) conversing inside the gate of the palace courtyard (105x83 mm.) on al and b2; (2) a Queen (Isabella) in her bed-chamber and Death (with a long arrow in his right hand) knocking at the door with his left (106x83 mm.) on a2^v; (3) a King and Queen (Ferdinand and Isabella) before a doorway (106x84 mm.) on b4; and (4) a King, a Queen and a young lady (Ferdinand, Isabella and Margaret) conversing inside the palace (108x85 mm.) on e7^v and e8^v. The fourth woodcut is thus found in both the inner and outer formes of the first sheet of the last quire [*or* same woodcut on e1.2.7.8(o) and (i)].

The Dialogues deal with the death of Don Juan, the only son of King Ferdinand and Queen Isabella and the husband of Princess Margaret of Austria. He died of a fever at Salamanca on the fourth of October, 1497 (cf. William H. Prescott, *History of the Reign of Ferdinand and Isabella*, London, 1867, II, 82). This is the date that appears on b1^v.

The only copy recorded is in the Pierpont Morgan Library (*Check List* no. 1706A). It measures 213x145 mm. and is bound in modern red morocco. An early MS note on folio 3 verso explains the phrase "Pesulum ostio appositum est" in the text. Obtained at the sale of the library of C. W. Dyson Perrins (Sotheby & Co., 5 November 1946, lot 516).

Assuming that this book had been fully and accurately described before and that the author and the title were well known, the following heading would suffice: "Ramírez, Diego. 1459-1537. Dialogi quattuor." Under such circumstances, also, the *contents* would consist of synoptic titles (or summaries) of the texts in place of the quasi-facsimile reproductions. If the information conveyed under *notes* had already been fully brought out in other descriptions, it would not be absolutely necessary to report this information again. Comments and observations derived from the comparison of several copies of a work would normally constitute the major portion of this section (here, of course, we are dealing with a unique book) and the location of these other copies listed in the next paragraph.

As will be seen in comparing this description with any of the standard ones in the *Gesamtkatalog*, the present account differs in minor points of detail from GW. For example, the GW only describes a maximum of three texts in its facsimile reproductions. When more texts are present only the opening lines of the first text and the closing lines of the last are reproduced, the other texts being noted in a contents list. Again, I have not differentiated between long and short *s* and the two forms of *r*, since it does not seem to me worth the trouble to include such *minutiae*. I am also not entirely convinced that it is important to note the number of lines to the full page for each leaf of a volume, particularly if it is a very large book; it might be quite sufficient to count the lines on just one characteristic page, duly indicating this information. Such details must be left to the wishes of the individual bibliographer and the nature of each particular book.

Dr. Greg was, of course, fully cognizant of the possibility that his formulary might not "prove equally suitable in detail to other fields," as he himself has said (p. 366). It is not to indulge in petty fault-finding that these further notes are appended, but solely to point out in exactly what circumstances the formulary will not work and where modifications will be needed in order to create a universally practicable shorthand (as desirable for the incunabulist as for the bibliographer of any other period).

On p. 368, Dr. Greg states: "Further, the exact form and fount of a signature are seldom if ever significant in the period with which I am familiar." Again (p. 377) Dr. Greg adds that signatures "may, for instance, be distinguished by the use of different type (though the cases are rare and doubtful)." This requires reconsideration, however, since different founts are used to distinguish signatures in early books. Specifically we find lombards duplicating gothic and roman letters in many Breviaries (BMC II:384-386), Diurnales (GW 8558), Missals (BMC V:541) and elsewhere (GW 3580 and 7839). Such a work as the Complutensian Bible (Alcala, 1514-1517) employs a number of different founts and sizes in the signatures. Again, a peculiarity of sixteenth-century Dutch liturgical books is that one finds signatures printed in red duplicating those in black (Nijhoff-Kronenberg 496, 497, 3536, 3537, etc.). In some books there are special notations and symbols to distinguish duplicating signatures, as in BMC V:559 (IB 24475) "aa[10] iterū aa[8] iterū bb[8] bb[8]" and in Polain 3573 "tt[8] tt.[8] tt:[8] tt.:[8] tt.:.[8] and tt.:..[8]". Occasionally a curved "d" (δ) is found in addition to a straight "d" (GW 5311, 7046, etc.). Such cases might simply be treated as repeated signatures (but for "χ" see text).

The statement (p. 369) that "no verso page ever bears a signature" is not quite correct since instances of this can be produced (BMC II:466-IA 8132 and GW 4810—PML 1652). These are fortunately sufficiently rare so that they may be treated as exceptional. Most Hebrew books are, of course, signed on the recto of the leaf according to the Semitic style of reading, but I suspect that there may be some printed by Christian printers and signed in a way familiar to their binders; if there be any such cases, the signatures would appear on the verso of the (Hebrew) leaf.

Dr. Greg's suggestion that alphabets which are doubled, trebled, etc., be abbreviated to 2A, 3A and so on (for AA, AAA, etc.) is perfectly satisfactory but not so his notation (p. 373):

But when an upper-case alphabet is doubled, A may become either AA or Aa—usually the latter. It is possible that printers occasionally distinguished between AA and Aa; but if so the instances are too few to deserve recognition, and in practice we ignore them.

Among incunabula, as Dr. Greg was aware, such different doublings are often differentiated (less frequently intermixed, this probably leading to no confusion—cf. GW 3566). Both Aa and AA are found in many volumes (GW 4275, 4290, 4292, 8540, 8556, 9160, etc.), as well as aa and aA (GW 4286) and aA and AA (*ibid.*). In Polain 1593, the signatures run: A-G, a-z, aa-gg, A-Z, aA-nN, aa-zz, Aa-Zz, AA-DD. Cowley (p. 98) has suggested that the form of doubling may be indicated, where gatherings run A-Z, Aa-Zz, Aaa-Zzz, Aaaa-Zzzz, as A-Z, Aa-Zz, 3A-3Z, 4A-4Z, but this will clearly not solve the problem where many different forms of doubling are encountered. Several special considerations may be mentioned. Where doubled letters occur without the corresponding single ones (as in Polain 3085) will it be necessary to remark on the absence of the single forms? What can be done about a book like GW 4294, where the signatures (in still another method of doubling) run: Aa-Az, Ba-Bz, Ca-Cg, Da-Dz, Ea-Es and Et. It should also be pointed out that in those cases where doubled (or tripled—see H 1418, BMC I:292) letters precede single ones, as in Polain 3355, 3412 and especially 3637, the use of the shorthand reference will not facilitate finding the leaf unless one has the full collation at hand.

Finally, there are a number of incunabula where Greg's formulary can be employed only with the greatest difficulty—perhaps, I do not understand it sufficiently. See, for example, GW 3538, 5424(5), 6598, 7693 and 9254, as well as Polain 2742, 3848, 3937 and 3944 (for later, non-English, books, cf. JCBL, III, 172 and 283). And, for such bibliographical monstrosities as GW 4282 and BMC VI:736 (Mombritius), it seems impossible to devise any satisfactory shorthand. The former, for example, uses only eight letters (a-h) as signatures, but b occurs 27 times and 29 c's are present; the quires run: a, then 9 b's, no c, then 7 d's, followed by a, then 9 d's, etc. If, as BMC (I:92) suggests, these marks refer to the presses—they certainly were useless for the binder—it implies that Rusch possessed at least seven, and perhaps eight, presses, a very considerable number (compare Haebler, *Inkunabelkunde*, pp. 62-63). We must then assume that the work was very unevenly distributed, since the presses represented by letters a-c printed just twice as many quires as those which used the letters e-g.

The variety of forms of signatures found in fifteenth-century books is so considerable that it will probably be a matter of some difficulty to suggest a satisfactory shorthand for their description. There are, however, other suggestions made by Dr. Greg which can be usefully employed in the description or discussion of incunabula. The symbol $\$$ for *any*, as well as *every*, signature is a very handy one, and so too is (o) for the outer and (i) for the inner form. The *minus* and *plus* signs to designate cancellation and replacement of leaves will save much pointless repetition. Thus $\$^4(^{\pm}\$2)$ can be safely used where the second leaf of a quire has been canceled and replaced by another leaf.

The shorthand unfortunately fails to provide for those rather numerous cases (among fifteenth-century books anyway) where cancellation in the usual sense did not take place but where leaves or quires were reprinted for other reasons. Thus, as in the well-known example of the 42-line Bible (see BMC I:17 and George P. Winship, *Printing in the Fifteenth Century*, Philadelphia, 1940, pp. 22-26), quires were sometimes reprinted when it was decided, in the course of printing, to increase the size of the edition. Again, in the case of the Greek *Horae* (Venice: Aldus, 1497), quire κ appears in two settings which are clearly not the result of cancellation but of some disturbance or miscalculation in the printing-office (cf. *PBSA*, XXXVI (1941), 24-26). On occasion, it is impossible to determine which was the immediate cause for the variant setting, as in the case of Wynkyn de Worde's edition of the *Constitutiones Provinciales* (see my paper in *Bookmen's Holiday*, pp. 470-474). It would be most useful to have some way of distinguishing between such different settings without the awkward and cumbersome methods now in use, such as "quire [1]-3rd setting." The *sigla* assigned by individual bibliographers, of course, are satisfactory for special studies but, on a broader scope, are useless and confusing when scholars do not employ the same symbols for the identical settings. It would be most happy if this difficulty could be resolved in a simple and satisfactory manner.

EARLY ENGLISH LITERATURE
1475-1700

James G. McManaway
The Folger Shakespeare Library

EARLY ENGLISH LITERATURE
1475-1700

WHEN the bibliographer turns from incunabula to the English book printed between 1475 and 1701, his sensations may be likened to those of a navigator in the time of Christopher Columbus who, leaving behind him the landlocked waters of the Mediterranean Sea, sailed between the Pillars of Hercules into the tumultuous and largely uncharted Atlantic Ocean. No longer does he have the equivalent of Hain's *Repertorium bibliographicum*, the British Museum *Catalogue of Books Printed in the XVth Century*, and the initial volumes of the *Gesamtkatalog der Wiegendrucke* to guide him in dealing with ninety per cent of the books to be described—though of course the few English books printed before 1501 can be and are bibliographically described as incunabula. On the contrary, the great majority of the books in the later field have not been given bibliographical attention.

English books from 1475 to 1640 are with a few exceptions listed among the more than 26,000 items in the invaluable *Short-title Catalogue*[1] compiled by Pollard, Redgrave, and others for the Bibliographical Society; and the three volumes of Dr. Wing's *Short-Title Catalogue of Books from 1641 to 1700*[2] will afford a modicum of information about the huge output of English presses, some 90,000 items, for the years 1641 to 1700. But only a small percentage of these books have received adequate bibliographical description. Thanks chiefly to the preoccupation of scholars with Shakespeare, his predecessors, contemporaries, and successors, the group of books which may be denominated English Renaissance drama has fared best of all. Dr. Greg's monumental *Bibliography of the English Printed Drama to the Restoration*,[3] which is based on a personal examination of, or on qualified reports on, every traceable copy of every edition, issue and state,[3a] is as nearly definitive as such a work can be. No other group of books has been nearly so fortunate. Of the bibliographies of particular authors, Professor Francis R. Johnson's *Critical Bibliography of the Works of Edmund Spenser*,[4] is among the best, though the early editions of Spenser's predecessor John Bale,[5] of his later contemporaries Samuel Daniel,[6] Thomas Heywood,[7] John Donne,[8] and of several authors of still later date, notably Robert Boyle,[9] Thomas Fuller,[10] and John Dryden,[11] have been described with varying degrees of merit. As might be expected, "the Printed Editions of the Holy Scripture"[12] have been minutely recorded, but the bibliography is not definitive. The large group of books known as Americana has been of such absorbing interest to historians and cartographers, as well as to booksellers and collectors, that we are not surprised to find occasional catalogues of the high quality of that compiled by George Watson Cole of the E. D. Church collection,[13] and they deserve mention here even though they include incunabula and other books that do not come within the scope of our subject. The catalogue of the great Arents Tobacco Library[14] is a mine of information. Of a wholly different sort are the bibliographies of books from a single press, such as De

Ricci's *Census of Caxtons*[15]; books printed in one city, such as Falconer Madan's *Oxford Books*[16]; and books printed in one country, such as Dickson and Edmond's *Annals of Scottish Printing*.[17] And much bibliographical assistance can be secured from yet another category of books, the catalogues of particular libraries, such as that of Bibles in the John Rylands Library[18] and the magnificent *Catalogue of the Carl H. Pforzheimer Library*.[19] This list is not exhaustive; it is intended merely to suggest some of the types of bibliographical work already in existence and to indicate how much remains to be done, as well as the great diversity of purposes that have motivated the compilers, and the varying degrees of completeness and finality that have been achieved.

It should be readily apparent that one set of standards is required for a check-list, another for the catalogue of a particular collection, and still another for an exhaustive analytical bibliography. And it should be equally obvious that these standards ought not to be confused. Thus the STC attempts to record briefly what books exist in a given period and to locate a few copies in English and American libraries for the convenience of readers. The Church Catalogue of Americana describes the particular copy of each book in the library in question. But a definitive bibliography, whether of an author, a press, or a *genre* should be based on the minute examination of every extant copy of the books in question.

An important difference should be noted between the initial motivation of the bibliographers of incunabula on the one hand and of sixteenth- and seventeenth-century English books on the other. The primary desire of the early bibliographers of incunabula was to discover and record the history of printing, to list surviving examples, to determine in what city each book was printed, who the printer was, and when the book was published. Many of the early bibliographers of English books of the sixteenth and seventeenth century began with an interest in literary and textual problems, and, chiefly with a view to solving these problems, resorted to the use of some of the techniques of the incunabulists or developed new ones of their own. This sweeping statement is, of course, an over-simplification of the facts, but surely it is not without significance that when the distinguished bibliographer of fifteenth-century books, Alfred W. Pollard, turned his attention to the later period and in *Shakespeare Folios and Quartos*[20] utilized some of the techniques of the incunabulist, it was the students of Shakespeare's text who seized the new tools Pollard put in their hands and began to secure results of such importance that 1909, the year of publication, may be taken as the starting point of modern, scientific bibliography.

It is ironical that, although R. B. McKerrow and Dr. Greg, who have contributed most to the development of bibliographical studies, were primarily interested in literary and textual problems, the scholars who have followed in their bibliographical train are frequently regarded by their colleagues with a sort of condescension, because of their supposed indifference to esthetic values and literary history. The bibliographer's insistence upon the importance of "the study of books as material objects irrespective of their contents"[21] is linked with his conviction that "in the ultimate resort the object of bibliographical study is . . . to reconstruct for each particular book the history of its life, to make it reveal in its most intimate detail the story of its birth and adventures as the material vehicle of the living word." Dr. Greg, whose words I have quoted, does not rest here. He reminds us that "bibliographical details may help to establish the relation of several editions of a printed book to one another"; "that this relation [is] itself a bibliographical fact"; and "that just as behind all the extant manuscripts lay the original that it was the object of [Lachmann's] genealogical method to reconstruct, so behind the earliest edition of a work lay the copy that the printer had before him, and that a good deal can sometimes be inferred respecting the character of this copy from the bibliographical and textual peculiarities of the editions printed from it." At this point Dr. Greg observes that "bibliography and textual criticism appear to interlock in a manner that makes it difficult if not impossible to separate their respective fields and leads one to wonder whether it may not in the end be necessary to bring most textual criticism within the province of bibliography."

The bibliographer's approach to the description of a book should be in terms of the printing craft. This fact was immediately recognized by the incunabulists, who concentrated upon the minute study of types and developed to a high degree that branch of bibliography which is called typography. Bibliographers of the later period have done comparatively little in this field, though Colonel Frank Isaac's three books on English and Scottish types serve as an excellent foundation for future study.[22]

Another phase of investigation that has suffered neglect is the paper on which the books were printed. As long ago as 1908, Dr. Greg's interest in the watermarks in the paper of certain Shakespeare quartos led him to the conclusion that a number of the quartos were falsely dated.[23] M. Briquet facilitated the identification of watermarks by putting at our disposal the results of his examination of thousands of sheets of paper in the Public Record Office in London.[24] Much remains undiscovered, however, about the sizes of paper used in the sixteenth and seventeenth centuries. For example, one copy of Sir John Harington's translation of *Orlando Furioso* (1591), a folio, is known in which the chain lines run perpendicular to the spine, as in a normal quarto; and several play quartos contain leaves in which the chain lines run as in an octavo. Furthermore, not all paper had watermarks. This phenomenon is particularly noticeable in the Restoration quarto plays, but it may be observed as early as 1622-1623, for in his essay on the printing of *Romeo and Juliet* and *Troilus and Cressida* in the First Folio, Dr. Giles E. Dawson discovered that in eight of the thirteen Folger copies of this book in which leaves gg1 and gg2 are demonstrably conjugate there is no watermark in either leaf.[25]

More attention has been devoted to the intricacies and idiosyncrasies of books printed from hand-set type on a hand press. However, so few people have had actual experience with the processes of hand printing that even today there is controversy about some of the details. Only a year or two ago Professor R. C. Bald was able to demonstrate that Elizabethan printers did not customarily hang up sheets printed on one side so that they might dry before being perfected[26]—thus correcting a widespread misapprehension that had the sanction of the late R. B. McKerrow. And one of the topics now most actively discussed by bibliographers is the precise method or methods by which early printers pulled and corrected proofs and how they integrated this process with the orderly machining of the other sheets of an edition.

With the unique Folger fragment of *The Passionate Pilgrim* in mind, I suggest that skilled bibliographers will familiarize themselves, likewise, with a related craft, that of bookbinding. It will be recalled that the most expert evaluation of the textual variants between the Folger fragment and the generally accepted first edition of the *Passionate Pilgrim* failed to determine the relative priority of the two editions, though printed one from the other in the same printing shop.[27] The probability that the unique Folger fragment represented the first edition was only established after my minute examination of the Burton volume containing the fragment disclosed certain previously unknown facts about the sewing and binding of the fragment and the four other little books of amorous verse bound with it, and thus recovered a vital part of the history of the text of the *Passionate Pilgrim*.[28] Every bibliographer could, in my opinion, be more confident that he has observed all the essential details and interpreted them correctly if he had himself sewed and bound in traditional fashion several books of varying sizes.

Equipped with a thorough knowledge of these and

other ancillary methods of investigating books as the physical vehicle of transmitting literary texts, to adapt Dr. Greg's phrases, a scholar is prepared to undertake the enumeration and description that are the foundations of bibliography. His intention will be

the formulary description of a series of books within a unified subject so that the relations of their texts are clarified and the method of publication of each individual volume is determined.[29]

It is about the means of attaining these high objectives that discussion rages. A scanning of the better bibliographies now in existence discloses that there are almost as many methods as bibliographers; and while the dictum attributed to A. W. Pollard that "it does not much matter what form you give to your bibliographical statement provided you make your intentions perfectly clear" is widely current, it is not to me entirely satisfactory. Since the publication of R. B. McKerrow's *Introduction to Bibliography* in 1927,[30] experiments have been conducted by many investigators in the recording of bibliographical data and in the solution of bibliographical problems. Perhaps enough time has now elapsed for bibliographers to take stock and to consider the desirability of setting up and adhering to certain standards and conventions of bibliographical description.

The primary requisite, surely, is the general agreement that the purpose of a bibliography is to describe the ideal copy of each book after the examination of every surviving copy of the book in question. By "ideal copy" is meant the book in the precise state in which the publisher intended it to be put on sale as complete and perfect. Such an ideal copy may contain cancels of leaves or quires, paste-on cancel slips, inserted prefatory matter or commendatory verses, or other special features, produced by changes in the intention of the author or the publisher or even by the intervention of authority. But all the departures from the original make-up of the book should have occurred during the course of continued printing and before the publisher rested from his labor to produce a perfect book. Many, perhaps most, books came on the market without untoward event and present no difficulties, but the production of a few—and these by far the most interesting—was attended by such deviousness or haste, by such good or evil fortune, or by such intensity of passion, as betrays itself in irregularities or abnormalities of collation. It is the function of the bibliographer to observe and record these phenomena, and by reconstructing the processes of the printer to recover the history of the text. Thus a careful study of the surviving copies of the quarto of *Henry IV*, Part 2, has put an end to much of the controversy that had continued since 1843 about the significance of the cancel in quire E.[31] There are two issues of this quarto. The first is normal in every respect, each full quire consisting of four leaves. The second issue differs from it in only one respect. In it, the original leaves E3 and E4 have been canceled and replaced by a full sheet of four leaves, the first three of which are signed E3, E4, and E5. The purpose of the cancel is to supply the text of Act III, Scene 1, which was not included in the first issue. A minute examination of the headlines, of the spelling and punctuation, and of the paper, reveals that the cancel was printed a short time after the completion of the presswork on the final half-sheet of the quarto. Since no changes were made in the title-page, it is clear that the publisher did not rest in his efforts to produce a complete and perfect book until he had inserted the cancel and, moreover, that he considered the cancel a part of the original book. The ideal copy of this quarto is, then, the copy that contains the cancel. And a definitive bibliography of the early editions of Shakespeare should so describe this ideal copy, as not only to record the physical facts of the printing of the book, but also to permit a reader to ascertain the details in which a particular copy deviates from this norm. Once the ideal copy of each edition, issue, and state has been determined, it becomes possible to evaluate the merits of any copy under examination and to relate it to other printings of the text.

My attempt to elucidate the meaning of the term "ideal copy" suggests the second requisite, namely, the establishment of a uniform terminology. In the STC, two copies of a book which differ in date or which name different publishers or booksellers are listed as belonging to separate issues, even though the changes may have been produced by stop-press correction. These criteria may be useful to many different users of books, but since the change usually occurred in the course of continuous printing, conservative bibliographers may well prefer to describe the books as belonging to variant states of the same issue. By reliance upon the principle of continuous printing it is even possible to argue plausibly that certain books with cancel title-pages do not belong to a different issue, for the reason that in the original printing an otherwise blank leaf at the end[32] was printed as an alternate title-page, thus producing books with two title-pages. Some copies will retain the title-page that was printed in the normal position; others will have the alternate title-page substituted in its place; and a few redundant copies may survive with both title-pages. Many other complications exist, but the citation of these two will be enough, I hope, to illustrate my belief that there is urgent need for a sound terminology and for a precise definition of terms, particularly of state, issue, and edition.

The third requisite is a generally accepted formulary of collation. It is not my intention to propose an ideal formulary or even to debate the advantages of using inferential signatures, of assigning the Greek character π to an unsigned preliminary gathering or the letter χ to an interpolated leaf or gathering. Several systems of notation[33] and many variants are now in use, with the result that the printed collation of a book may be intelligible only to the man who wrote it. The purpose of a collational formula is to describe concisely the physical make-up of a book. That description should be as brief as is consistent with completeness, and it should be incapable of misinterpretation. Where would physicists and astronomers be if mathematical notation were subject to the variation of whim or personal preference? It is my belief that the task of describing bibliographically the thousands of English books in the period 1475 to 1700 will be greatly facilitated by the acceptance of a standard system of notation.

This system should not be absolutely rigid, nor should

it be so complex as to attempt to provide for every conceivable aberration. There will always be difficult books, comparable to the hard legal cases that make bad law. So it will always be necessary to write explanatory notes in order to give a full account of the printing of some books. On the other hand, it should be recognized that collational formulae are a kind of shorthand, written by experts for the use of experts; so there is every reason for refusing to cater to the supposed limitations of "the intelligent reader." Concise, unambiguous notation is indispensable both in formal bibliographies and for purposes of reference in all other learned publications.

The problems that arise in the transcription of title-pages are well known, and so are the conventional solutions. My own preference is for quasi-facsimile transcriptions, with notation of swash capitals and with full information about rules, borders, and ornaments or publishers' devices. The statement of format is not difficult until odd sizes of paper rob the conventional terms of meaning. There are, however, certain other aspects of bibliography that were unknown to men like McKerrow or only dimly apprehended. They are related to printing-house practices that specialists are just now in process of investigating, and they are, I think, best dealt with in notes, following the collational formula.

One of the practices was described some years ago by Mr. W. A. Jackson as a result of his examination of copies of three seventeenth-century books.[34] One of these, Sir John Hayward's *The First Part of the Life and Raigne of King Henry IV*, as is well known,[35] was called in by the Bishop of London and ordered to be burned because of supposed parallels between events leading up to the deposition of King Richard II and contemporary events in the reign of Queen Elizabeth. Yet scores of copies of the book are extant. Comparison of types and ornaments revealed that these copies are what may be called seventeenth-century type facsimiles, the piratical printers of which sometimes went to extraordinary lengths to avoid detection.

In the course of examining books offered to the Folger Library for purchase and of assisting in the compilation of *A Check-List of English Plays, 1641-1700,* I have come upon evidence of several other printing house practices that are not well known. These relate to the storage of type for use in the printing of a later edition.[36] An instructive example is *The Kings Maiesties Declaration to his Subjects Concerning lawfull Sports to bee vsed,* printed by Robert Barker, the King's Printer, in 1633, one copy of which came to the Folger in the Harmsworth purchase, a second copy being acquired in October 1945. These two books were printed throughout from identical type; but an ornamental initial in one copy has been replaced in the other, and enough page numbers, signatures and catchwords have been reset to prove that after Barker completed printing the first edition, he stripped the forms and then tied up the type pages and held them for reimposition and the printing of a second edition.

Barker's purpose is not easy to discover. His book was printed at a time when the number of copies of an ordinary book that might be printed from one setting of type was strictly limited, in order to balance the employment of pressmen and compositors. The order of 1588 provided that not more than 1,250 or 1,500 copies of any book might be run off at "one ympression" except "grammers, Accidences, prymers, and Catechismes," of which the number might be 2,500 or 3,000, and "except also the statutes and proclamacons with all other bookes belonging to ye office of her maiesties printer which by reason of her maiesties affayres are to be limited to no number."[37] Since as king's printer Barker could print official publications in editions of any desired size, it may be assumed that when he found himself unable to guess how many copies of this controversial *Declaration* might be required he completed the first printing, rinsed and tied up his type, and awaited developments. When the demand for additional copies was sufficient, he was able to put out a second impression without the expense of resetting his type. In such books as this there is little, if anything, in a single copy to arouse the suspicions of a bibliographer; only when several copies can be placed side by side do the tantalizing differences begin to appear.

Another book of the same period falls into a different category from that of Barker's official publication, the anonymously compiled and published *Depositions and Articles against Thomas Earle of Strafford*, 1640. One of the Folger copies is from the Harmsworth Library; the second was acquired in 1939; and the third I bought in 1945, because I noted that with the exception of a few lines on one title-page and of several pages of text these three books were printed from one setting of the type of the text, with differences only in head ornaments, rules, catchwords, and other elements outside the type pages.

Printers appear to have been able to tie securely a solid block of type but to have had difficulty with the furniture and such appurtenances as headlines, signatures, rules, and ornaments.[38] The small amount of resetting that may be observed in the two reissues of this book was probably necessitated by the accidental pieing of type. It should be noted that the trial of the Earl was a *cause celèbre* and that the book enjoyed a sensational popularity. What deal the printer made with his compositors cannot be known, but surely he must have recompensed them in some way, for, unlike the authorities, they could hardly have been deceived.

James Shirley's *Triumph of Peace* illustrates a third type of situation that tempted publishers to resort to illegal measures involving the reimposition of standing type. This masque was produced in 1634 as a rebuke to William Prynne and the Puritans for their criticism of the court, and was performed by the gentlemen of the four Inns of Court. To advertise and introduce the festivities, there was a triumphant parade from Holborn to Whitehall.

Behind Marshal Darrel (of the pamphleteer's own Inn!) and his twenty torch-bearers rode the hundred handsomest men of the four Inns, gloriously clad, perfectly mounted, and attended by three hundred pages and lackeys. Then for contrast came a troop of beggars on decrepit nags. Then followed troops of song birds, of caricatured monopolists, of owls. Interspersed were bands of English, Scotch, French, Italian, and German musicians, forty lutes playing in unison, to furnish one of the greatest musical demonstrations England had known. Finally came gorgeous chariots bearing the masquers, their silks and satins ruddy in the light of flambeaux.[39]

To take full advantage of the masque's astounding popularity, the text of the *Triumph of Peace*[40] was printed at once by John Norton for William Cooke, and when eager customers flocked in to buy, page after page of the first setting of type was fitted with new headlines, signatures and catchwords, and reimposed—both to save time, I imagine, and to avoid the cost of resetting the type. Meanwhile the author made some changes in his text, or else the printer was supplied with a more ample and accurate version, for there are numerous revisions and resettings in the midst of reimposed pages of the first setting. Other entertainments may be cited in the publication of which the temptation to hurry into circulation an exceptionally large edition led to evasion of the regulations.[41]

More than one Restoration play may be instanced in which extensive sections of type were reimposed, such as Thomas Durfey's *Richmond Heiress* (1693). Some of these books can hardly be differentiated by even the most exact transcription of the title-pages. One title-page may differ from another only in having a slender rule substituted for a thick one, or a crooked rule for a straight. That these are not simple press corrections can be proved by the concomitant changes in the elements that occur in the margins of the book, outside the letter-press of the text. In the case of several plays, such as Shirley's masque *The Triumph of Peace*, the signs of reimposition are observed most readily in the location of signatures and in the shape and spacing of the parentheses that enclose the page numbers.

Textual editors long ago adopted the maxim that the

unit of study is the form; but in describing the three groups of books I have just been discussing, bibliographers must adopt as their unit of comparison the letter-press of each individual page, and they must bear constantly in mind the possibility that accidents in the handling of blocks of standing type reserved for reimposition may require the identification of units even smaller than the page.

Experiences with books like these just mentioned confirm me in my belief that the scholar who would compile an analytical bibliography must examine personally every extant copy of the books in question or accurate reproductions of them. Some of the details of the books that require more attention than has hitherto been given them are headlines, signatures, catchwords, rules and ornaments. The only notable deficiency of Dr. Greg's *Bibliography of the English Drama to the Restoration* is its inadequate account of headlines. In this *Bibliography,* condensed statements provide data about changes in the spelling and punctuation of running titles, but in the future more will be required. There should be exact measurement of the running titles and minute examination of the type so that the bibliographer can ascertain and record how many skeleton forms were used and in what order they recur. Any deviations from the pattern are clues to irregularities in the printing of the book.

The use of headlines in the solution of bibliographical problems seems to have begun, as did so many other phases of bibliographical study, with A. W. Pollard, who in *Shakespeare Folios and Quartos* (1909) traced somewhat sketchily the periodic recurrence of certain headlines and also certain of the brass rules that box the headlines and frame the two columns of text of the First Folio and suggested a few of the conclusions that might be drawn from a more careful examination of the book.[42] Twenty years passed before the problem was attacked seriously in a study[43] that three years later was expanded into a full-length reconstruction of the history of the printing of the First Folio.[44]

Headlines were mentioned incidentally for a number of years,[45] but nothing of importance was added until in an attempt to solve a textual problem in *The Roaring Girl* by Middleton and Dekker I had occasion to work out a technique that permitted the determination of the authoritative readings in a twice-printed passage of text.[46] While the inner form of sheet I of this play was being printed, an accident occurred that resulted in the pieing of a part of the type. In resetting this type, numerous variants were introduced, some of which appear esthetically superior to the original readings. The crucial point was to distinguish between the first and the second settings of type. This it was possible to do irrefutably by discovering that Nicholas Okes, the supposed printer, followed a definite pattern in his use of headlines in the quarto, and that in the Folger, Dyce, and Pforzheimer copies the proper headlines appear in the inner form of sheet I. In the other extant copies, two new headlines make their first appearance in this form. Furthermore the new headlines are found regularly thereafter in their appointed places in all copies of the quarto. Obviously the readings which occur in company with the substituted headlines in inner I are lacking in authority, whereas the other readings derive from the manuscript copy.

Valuable papers by Professors Bowers and Hinman, Mr. Wolf, and others have followed in rapid succession,[47] and all bibliographers are now aware of the importance of scrutinizing headlines.

The Restoration plays in which reimposition of type occurs frequently have only pagination in the headlines. It is my untested hypothesis that variations in the headlines that accompany reimposition of stored or standing type may best be detected by measuring the distance from the inner margin of the letterpress to the first character or numeral in the pagination, and also measuring the width of the numerals, including the parentheses or square brackets that may enclose them.[48] This is a refinement that I have not observed in any bibliography. Unless a simpler and equally dependable technique can be devised, future bibliographers may have to compile these tedious, and often voluminous, statistics.

At this point it may be well to suggest that bibliographers in the field of English Renaissance books will be wise to imitate the incunabulists in recording the measurements of blocks of twenty lines of type, and that perhaps they should also record the height of the type page, with and without the headlines, et cetera, that lie outside the text.

Another practice deserves at least a passing reference, that of half-sheet imposition. McKerrow[49] wrote that no example of it in sixteenth-century English printing had come to his attention, but several years ago Dr.

W. H. Bond described such a book,[50] and it has been suggested that the first edition of the *Merchant of Venice* is another.[51] In the Restoration period, and probably during the interregnum, printers had frequent recourse to this technique. The bibliographer must be alert for instances of half-sheet imposition and record them.

There are many bibliographical problems which I have not mentioned, and only a glancing allusion has been given to others. I hope there is no disappointment that I have not attempted to present a systematic treatise or detailed formularies of collation; the subject matter would have proved refractory and the time too short. Instead I have indicated some of the problems of the bibliographer in the field of English books, 1475-1700, which differ from those of the incunabulist, described a few of the more recently developed bibliographical techniques, and suggested several new lines of investigation that deserve the attention of critical bibliographers.

It is my belief that in the twenty years since the publication of McKerrow's *Introduction to Bibliography* there has been enough experimentation for us to hope that within five more years, when McKerrow's book will have reached its twenty-fifth anniversary, several comprehensive treatises will have been published, one of which by its simplicity and reasonableness and by its high standards, will so impose itself on bibliographers that its terminology and formulae will be generally adopted both here and abroad. Then, unless the curse of Babel rests upon us, we shall all speak the same bibliographic language, more or less as scientists speak the same mathematical language.

Notes

1. A. W. Pollard and G. R. Redgrave, *A Short-title Catalogue of Books Printed in England, Scotland & Ireland and of English Books Printed Abroad, 1475-1640*, London, 1926.

2. Donald Wing, *Short-title Catalogue of Books Printed in England, Scotland, Ireland, Wales, and British America and of English Books Printed in Other Countries, 1641-1700*, vol. I, New York, 1945.

3. W. W. Greg, *A Bibliography of the English Printed Drama to the Restoration*, vol. I, London, 1939.

3a. Plays, especially reprints, that have survived in numerous copies, have not been sought outside the principal British and American libraries; privately owned items are included if they are unique or excessively rare.

4. Francis R. Johnson, *A Critical Bibliography of the Works of Edmund Spenser Printed before 1700*, Baltimore, 1933.

5. W. T. Davies, "A Bibliography of John Bale," *Oxford Bibliographical Society Proceedings & Papers*, V (1936-1939), 201-279.

————, "Additions and Corrections," *ibid.*, new series; I, fasc. i (1948), pp. 44-45.

6. H. Sellers, "A Bibliography of the Works of Samuel Daniel 1585-1623, with an Appendix of Daniel's Letters," *Oxford Bibliographical Society Proceedings & Papers*, II (1927-1930), 29-54.

————, "Supplementary Note to A Bibliography of the Works of Samuel Daniel," *ibid.*, pp. 341-342.

7. A. M. Clark, "A Bibliography of Thomas Heywood," *Oxford Bibliographical Society Proceedings & Papers*, I (1922-1926), 97-153.

8. Geoffrey Keynes, *A Bibliography of Dr* [sic] *John Donne, Dean of Saint Paul's*, Cambridge, 1932. Second edition.

9. J. F. Fulton, "A Bibliography of the Honourable Robert

Boyle, Fellow of the Royal Society," *Oxford Bibliographical Society Proceedings & Papers*, III (1931-1933), 1-172.

J. F. Fulton, "Addenda to a Bibliography of the Honourable Robert Boyle," *ibid.*, III (1931-1933), pp. 337-363.

————, "Second Addenda," *ibid.*, new series, I, fasc. i (1948), pp. 33-38.

10. Strickland Gibson, "A Bibliography of the Works of Thomas Fuller, D. D., With an Introduction by Geoffrey Keynes," *Oxford Bibliographical Society Proceedings & Papers*, IV (1934-1935), 63-161.

11. Hugh Macdonald, *John Dryden, a Bibliography of Early Editions, and of Drydeniana*, Oxford, 1939.

12. T. H. Darlow and H. F. Moule, *Historical Catalogue of the Printed Editions of Holy Scripture in the Library of The British and Foreign Bible Society*, London, 1903-1911.

13. George Watson Cole, *A Catalogue of Books Relating to the Discovery and Early History of North and South America Forming a Part of the Library of E. D. Church*, New York, 1907.

14. Jerome E. Brooks, *Tobacco, its History Illustrated by the Books, Manuscripts and Engravings in the Library of George Arents, Jr., together with an Introductory Essay, a Glossary and Bibliographical Notes*, New York, 1937-1943.

15. Seymour de Ricci, *A Census of Caxtons*, London, 1909. (The Bibliographical Society, *Illustrated Monograms*, no. 15.)

16. Falconer Madan, *Oxford Books, a Bibliography of Printed Works Relating to the University and City of Oxford, or Printed or Published There*, Oxford, 1895-1931.

17. Robert Dickson and John Philip Edmond, *Annals of Scottish Printing from the Introduction of the Art in 1507 to the Beginning of the Seventeenth Century*, Cambridge, 1890.

18. *The English Bible in the John Rylands Library, 1525-1640*, [London and Aylesbury] 1899.

19. *The Carl H. Pforzheimer Library, English Literature, 1475-1700*, New York, 1940.

20. Alfred W. Pollard, *Shakespeare Folios and Quartos, a Study in the Bibliography of Shakespeare's Plays, 1594-1685*, London, 1909.

21. W. W. Greg, "Bibliography—A Retrospect," in *The Bibliographical Society 1892-1942, Studies in Retrospect*, London, 1945, pp. 25, 27, etc.

22. Frank Isaac, *English & Scottish Printing Types, 1501-1535* 1508-1541*, London, 1930. (The Bibliographical Society, *Facsimiles and Illustrations*, no. II).

———, ———, *1535-1558* 1552-1558*, London, 1932. (The Bibliographical Society, *Facsimiles and Illustrations*, no. III.)

———, *English Printers' Types of the Sixteenth Century*. Oxford, 1936.

23. See "On Certain False Dates in Shakespearian Quartos," *Library*, 2d ser., IX (1908), 113-131; 381-409. Greg's conclusions were independently confirmed by the contemporaneous researches of W. J. Neidig—*cf*. his article in *Modern Philology*, VIII (1910-1911), 145-163.

24. C. M. Briquet, *Les filigranes, dictionnaire historique des marques du papier dès leur apparition vers 1282 jusqu'en 1600*, Leipzig, 1923. Second edition.

25. "A Bibliographical Problem in the First Folio of Shakespeare," *Library*, 4th ser., XXII (1941-1942), 25-33.

26. "Evidence and Inference in Bibliography," *English Institute Annual, 1941*, New York, 1942, pp. 159-183.

27. See Hyder E. Rollins: "The date of O 2 [the unique Folger fragment] is entirely conjectural, and whether it represents a second, or a first, edition remains for further study to determine." *A New Variorum Edition of Shakespeare, The Poems*, Philadelphia & London, 1938, pp. 526ff.

28. See *The Passionate Pilgrim*, ed. Joseph Quincy Adams, New York and London, 1939, pp. vii, xv-xxxvi.

29. Quoted from the manuscript of a treatise on analytical bibliography by Professor Fredson T. Bowers of the University of Virginia.

30. Ronald B. McKerrow, *An Introduction to Bibliography for Literary Students*, Oxford, 1927.

31. J. G. McManaway, "The Cancel in the Quarto of *2 Henry IV*," *University of Missouri Studies*, XXI (1946), 67-80. See also Professor John Dover Wilson's edition of the play in the "New Cambridge" edition, which appeared later in the year.

32. Thus in some copies of *A Preparation vnto Fasting and Repentance. By Peter Moulin, and translated by I. B. . . . London: Printed by T. S. for Nathaniel Newbery, and are to be sould at the signe of the Starre vnder S. Peters Church in Cornehill, and in Popes head ally. 1620.*, signed A^6, B-E^{12}; leaf E12 has exactly the same title and imprint as appears on A2 (leaf A1 is blank except for the signature), but is printed from a different setting of type. Differences in inking probably explain the apparent lack of a period after "S" in "S. Peters" on E12 and of the presence there of a hyphen in "Popes-head" that seems to be wanting on A2. The purpose of two settings of the title-page in this book is not readily apparent.

If there were no blank leaves at the end, the printer sometimes used a blank leaf that occurred elsewhere in the volume. See the Folger copy of a book by Michel Baudier, STC 1593, which has two different title-pages, one on A1 and another on A2. The title-page on A2 reads as follows: *The History of the Serrail, And of the Court of the Grand Seigneur, Emperour of the Turkes. Wherein is Seene the Image of the Othman Greatnesse, A Table of the humane passions, and the Examples of the inconstant prosperities of the Court. Translated out of French by Edward Grimeston Serjant at Armes. London, Printed by William Stansby.* Because of its position and its agreement with the running-title ("The History of the Serrail, and of the Court of the Grand Seigneur"), this is in all probability the original title-page.

The wording on A1 is very different, as is the imprint: *The History of the Imperiall Estate of the Grand Seigneurs: Their Habitations, Liues, Titles, Qualities, Exercises, Workes, Reuenewes, Habit, Discent, Ceremonies, Magnificence, Iudgements, Officers, Fauourites, Religion, Power, Gouernment and Tyranny. Translated out of French by E. G. S. A. London, Printed by William Stansby, for*

Richard Meighen, next to the middle Temple in Fleetstreet. 1635.
This title-page names the publisher as well as the printer and states
his place of business; it partially conceals the identity of the transla-
tor by substituting initials for his name and title; and, discarding the
unfamiliar word "Serrail," it gives a detailed listing of the exotic
contents of the book, calculated to catch the eye of the prospective
buyer. Any one of these changes may have been the reason for
printing a second title-page. I am indebted to my colleague, Dr. Paul
S. Dunkin, for the references to these two books, but he is not to be
held responsible for my comments on them.

33. See Alfred W. Pollard and W. W. Greg, "Some Points in
Bibliographical Descriptions," *Transactions of the Bibliographical
Society*, IX (1906-1909), 31-52.

F. Madan, "Degressive Bibliography," *ibid.*, pp. 53-65.

F. Madan, E. Gordon Duff, and S. Gibson, "Standard Descriptions of Printed Books," *Oxford Bibliographical Society Proceedings
& Papers*, I (1922-1926), 55-64.

R. B. McKerrow, *op. cit.*

Arundel Esdaile, *A Student's Manual of Bibliography*, London,
1931.

W. W. Greg, "A Formulary of Collation," *Library*, 4th ser., XIV
(1933-1934), 365-382.

J. D. Cowley, *Bibliographical Description and Cataloguing*, London, 1939.

Two other discussions should not be overlooked:

John Philip Edmond, *Suggestions for the Description of Books
Printed between 1501 and 1640*; reprinted from *The Library Asso-
ciation Record* for the members of the Bibliographical Society of
Lancashire, 1902.

George Watson Cole, "A Survey of the Bibliography of English
Literature, 1475-1620, with Especial Reference to the Work of the
Bibliographical Society of London," *Papers of the Bibliographical
Society of America*, XXIII (1929), 1-95.

34. W. A. Jackson, "Counterfeit Printing in Jacobean Times,"
Library, 4th ser., XV (1934-1935), 364-376.

35. E. P. Kuhl, "The Stationers' Company and Censorship (1599-1601)," *Library*, 4th ser., IX (1928-1929), 388-394; Margaret Dowling, "Sir John Hayward's Troubles over his *Life of Henry IV*," *ibid.*, XI (1930-1931), 212-224.

36. As in so many other bibliographical discussions, Dr. Greg is among the first to make a contribution—*cf.* his "Notes on Old Books," *Library*, 4th ser., III (1922-1923), 55-56, in which he cites the case of a portion of Abraham Cowley's *Works* that was kept in type from 1688 to 1693. See also McKerrow's *Introduction*, pp. 178-180.

37. "A Copie of certen orders concerning printing," in Edward Arber, ed., *A Transcript of the Registers of the Company of Stationers of London; 1554-1640 A.D.*, London, 1875, II, 43.

38. *Cf.* Otway's *Friendship in Fashion* (1678), the dedication of which seems to have been twice imposed. After the first imposition, the signature of the author on A2^v, which is separated from the text by a wide space, was removed before the type was tied up; similarly two rules at the top of A2 were put aside. When the type was reimposed, the rules were omitted and the author's name was replaced by his initials.

39. Alfred Harbage, *Cavalier Drama, an Historical and Critical Supplement to the Study of the Elizabethan and Restoration Stage*, New York, 1936, p. 17.

40. W. W. Greg has published a preliminary study of the peculiarities of this masque, "*The Triumph of Peace*, a Bibliographer's Nightmare," *Library*, 5th ser., I (1946-1947), 113-126.

41. It has been suggested by my colleague, Dr. Edwin E. Willoughby, that the variation in text, though slight, may have constituted a sufficient change to make the regulation inapplicable.

42. See pp. 134-137.

43. E. E. Willoughby, "A Note on the Typography of the Running Titles of the First Folio," *Library*, 4th ser., IX (1928-1929), 385-387.

44. E. E. Willoughby, *The Printing of the First Folio of Shakespeare*, Oxford, 1932. (Supplement to the Bibliographical Society's *Transactions*, no. 8).

45. See E. E. Willoughby's review of the Huntington Library facsimile of *Hamlet* (1603), in which he discusses recurring headlines as evidence that the printing of the quarto was uninterrupted— *Library Quarterly*, II (1932), 89-90. See also the review in *Modern Language Notes* XLIX (1934), 118-120, of Spencer's edition of Massinger's *Bondman*, in which I comment on the irregularity of the headlines in this quarto and their relation to the number of compositors and presses. In his bibliography of Spenser referred to above, Francis R. Johnson deals at some length with the headlines of the *Faerie Queene*, Q1.

46. "Thomas Dekker: Further Textual Notes," *Library*, 4th ser., XIX (1938-1939), 176-179.

47. See, for example, F. T. Bowers, "The Headline in Early Books, *English Institute Annual, 1941*, pp. 185ff., and Charlton Hinman, "New Uses for Headlines as Bibliographical Evidence," *ibid.*, pp. 207ff.

48. In his article, "New Uses for Headlines," just cited, Professor Hinman proposes such measurements as these as a quick means of identifying recurring headlines, but with no reference to their use in detecting cases of re-imposed type.

49. McKerrow, *Introduction*, pp. 66-70, remarks that examples can be recognized only by accident and postulates the kind of evidence that would prove half-sheet imposition. He makes no mention of headlines as a clue.

50. "Imposition by Half-sheets," *Library*, 4th ser., XXII (1941-1942), 163-167.

51. By Miss Margaret Brereton in her unpublished Master's essay submitted at the University of Maryland in 1941. Miss Brereton used headlines as evidence. See also F. T. Bowers, *English Institute Annual, 1941* (New York, 1942), pp. 199-205.

EARLY AMERICANA

Lawrence C. Wroth
The John Carter Brown Library

EARLY AMERICANA

IN THE sense in which we employ it in this inquiry the term "Americana" relates to that category of the printed book which has to do with the western hemisphere either by virtue of its subject, no matter what its place of publication, or by virtue of its publication in that hemisphere, no matter what its subject. The term enjoys broader employments than this in some circles, but at this moment we are not concerned with its application to American antiques or to the use of it as a designation for American folkways, songs, speech peculiarities, or the distinctive brand of pithy comment known as the wisecrack, the response of the wit of man in contact with American soil or the peculiar conditions of American life. Those who planned the present course of lectures employed in their announcement of this third and last of the series the still more restrictive term, "early" Americana. May we assume that they had in mind as the materials of our investigation books of the definition already given, printed before the year 1801?

In the nature of things the beginning date, the origin of the subject of Americana, was the year 1493, when in the month of April there was printed at Barcelona a single sheet folded, upon which in four pages of text in the Spanish language appeared for the first time in print Columbus' account of his discovery of certain islands in the western ocean, islands unknown to Ptolemy and consequently a new world to that generation of men. The category of materials we know as Americana is, therefore, relatively young, not yet five hundred years of age, but it was a lusty child from birth. In the course of the centuries it has grown tall and broad. Along with it, and to a very great extent because of it, has developed the stage of culture in which the world today has its being, the modern civilization which, for good or ill, frames the thoughts and actions of men and nations. Anyone interested in life must in the nature of things be interested in Americana.

The books which make up this category are a disordered, haphazard lot, issued normally without previously formed plan but with sharp, immediate purpose by men of many kinds and races. Their subjects are as many and as varied as the country they derive from is large. Among them are found in all their aspects geography, politics, science, war, religion, commerce, ethnography, the conflict of races, tyranny, revolt, imperialism, and democracy. The authors who created their content were rough sailors, priests, merchants, men of learning in many branches, soldiers bent upon conquest, land-hungry colonists, men in search of religious freedom, square pegs seeking, often in vain, holes into which they might fit, and honest or dishonest promoters. Their motives range the area between idealism and rawest materialism. Their books range in content and style from great literature, loftily conceived, to the merest claptrap; in physical form from noble typographical productions to lowly broadsides intended to be thrown away immediately after their matter had been read and comprehended.

This is an exciting literature to the imaginative man,

a great body of writing dealing with new lands and oceans, and strange, uncouth races, with the upthrust of young nations and vital political ideologies, with forces which, literally, altered the economy of the world. Through it all runs the bright thread of romance, for where there is conflict and effort and growth romance is inevitably present. This is an exciting literature and a literature created, without plan or order, upon impulse, through necessity, or through the need for personal or communal defense or aggression. For centuries men have realized that the literature thus come into being needed organization.

Though this literature has in it qualities which make it both superficially and fundamentally different from any other, we need not, for that reason, say that its organization requires a distinctive and unique bibliographical standard. That would not be true. It is true, however, or so it seems to me, that within the accepted bibliographical practice, the treatment of Americana demands a shift of emphasis. That affirmation, I believe, is the nub of my discourse.

Throughout the past three centuries there has occurred a slow advance toward an effective standard of organization and description of printed Americana. A brief review of some of the stages in this progression will provide us with background and, at the same time, bring into view certain fundamental components of the standard we are seeking.

In 1629 Antonio de León Pinelo published in a single quarto volume his *Epitome de la Biblioteca Oriental i Occidental,* a work concerned with listing for scholarly uses the existing printed and manuscript books on the new worlds of the East and the West. Under broad general classifications, he arranged his titles in an order roughly, though by no means consistently, chronological, entering them without care for the alphabet under the names of their authors, but bringing together his scattered elements in an author index and an index of anonymous titles. Before this time American bibliographies, with certain very minor exceptions, had been brief lists of titles compiled by conscientious historians and geographers to display their sources of information for a particular work, the "bibliography" or "list of references" which today is found customarily in serious compositions. León Pinelo attempted for the first time a general American bibliography, a *catalogue raisonné* of American source materials. Though he gave his readers the minimum in the way of collation or description, he presented them with an ordered plan of enduring usefulness. Upon that plan more than a century later Andrés Gonzáles de Barcia brought out in 1737-38, in three folio volumes, a great enlargement of León Pinelo's materials, retaining for the new work, quite inappropriately in the sense of size, the original designation, *Epitome de la Bibliotheca oriental, y occidental*. Barcia retained also the broad classifications of the original work, but threw his titles together hugger-mugger under the several heads without regard either to the alphabet or chronology. Like his predecessor, he translated his titles into Spanish and in other ways made his book a difficult one to use. By way of compensation for this lack of system, he provided a guide to his repertory in the form of an index of authors and titles. We cannot blame him if, like León Pinelo in the earlier work, he followed the Spanish custom of entering his authors in this index under their Christian names. The descriptions of the books he entered were of the scantiest. But we cannot leave Barcia the bibliographer without greater praise than these words seem to accord him. His *Epitome,* commonly referred to as Pinelo-Barcia, is still used, and the discussion of sources in his *Ensayo cronologico, para la Historia general de la Florida* is one of the earliest North American sectional bibliographies, still consulted with interest by historians and bookmen.

The earliest attempt in English to provide a general bibliography of Americana was the catalogue which Bishop White Kennett made of the library he formed and gave to the Society for the Propagation of the Gospel in Foreign Parts. The White Kennett library has a place set aside in the esteem of certain of us, because it was the prototype of the John Carter Brown Library in most essentials—in the intention of its creator, in the geographical scope of its interests, in its transfer *en bloc* to institutional ownership, and in the publication by its private owner of a chronologically arranged catalogue with an index of authors' names. We hope the analogy ends there. The slow dispersion through the centuries of the fine White Kennett library of Americana is one of the tragedies. Virtually its only monument today is the *Bibliothecae Americanae Primordia,* the work we know as the "White Kennett Catalogue." In this substantial volume were arranged chronologically the titles of some sixteen hundred books, pamphlets, and broadsides relating chiefly to the English colonies of North America, but varied and enriched by works on discovery and exploration and by works relating to the countries of Latin America. Our good scholarly bishop, a great collector, let us remember, gave us little in the way of collation in his catalogue entries. His sin of commission was of a more serious character, for he created scores of ghost books through the violence he did to titles in condensing them for reasons of space economy.

The truly uplifting event in the field of our review occurred when in 1866 Henry Harrisse published his *Bibliotheca Americana Vetustissima*. The B.A.V., as it has ever since been called, was a chronological listing of all books known to Harrisse relating to America, published in the period 1493-1550. Here, at last, the scholarly intelligence had been applied to the segregation, identification, description, and annotation of the basic printed sources concerning the New World in the periods of discovery and exploration. The chronological arrangement showing the development of the subject, the effort to transcribe titles fully and exactly with appended translations into English, comment upon the event or circumstances which brought the texts into being, and, finally, the location of copies established upon a new plane the bibliographical description of Americana. Harrisse's collations, it is true, leave much to be desired, and, a pioneer in his field, working in New York in the 1860's far from the great libraries of the world, he made many errors. Only those of us who are without sin in that respect may fairly criticize him.

But despite inexactness and defects in method, a new

bibliographical standard was set up by Harrisse in the B.A.V., and carried forward in his special study, *Notes pour servir à l'Histoire, à la Bibliographie et à la Cartographie de la Nouvelle-France,* published six years later. The revised John Carter Brown Catalogue, edited by John Russell Bartlett and published in 1875-1882, carried on with the Harrisse system even though it was an extensive compilation of over twenty-two hundred titles covering a period of more than two centuries. In the meantime, in 1868, two years after the publication of the B.A.V., Joseph Sabin began to issue his huge *Dictionary of Books relating to America.* Indispensable though that work has become, those of us who use it every day wish that its compiler had arranged his titles chronologically instead of alphabetically by authors' names. Sabin's decision to make a dictionary rather than a chronological catalogue was a step backward in the progress of American bibliography.

In *A Catalogue of . . . the Library of E. D. Church,* the work of George Watson Cole, the ideas underlying the B.A.V. were carried forward to an ideal difficult to attain under most circumstances the bibliographer is likely to encounter. Chronological arrangement was adopted, and the problem of title transcriptions was solved by the photographic reproduction of title-pages. With Harrisse the emphasis had been upon the compiler's comment on the book in hand, whereas with Dr. Cole the collations, more elaborate than any yet seen, outweighed the notes in importance. The service of this catalogue to the bibliographer's procedure has been beyond that of any similar work of our time.

The twentieth century introduced us to new interests —to the study of the output of local presses, for example, to greater and more refined bibliographical studies of places, persons, and subjects. Preëminent among the many works which record the production of local presses is the noble compilation of Charles Evans, a vast repertory in chronological arrangement of all available books printed in English America and the early United States. Its elaborate classified index, its index of authors and titles, and its lists of printers are laboriously compiled aids for which users of the book are forever grateful. In respect to collations and notes Evans is greatly inferior to the several extensive works in which José Toribio Medina, his Chilean contemporary, recorded in chronological arrangement many thousands of books proceeding from Mexico, Peru, Chile, and several lesser communities of Spanish America. Medina's titles were entered chronologically with complete transcriptions of their title-pages, with line-endings, collations, contents, references, locations of copies, notes biographical and bibliographical, and, following the catalogue, an index of the names of authors and persons mentioned in notes and titles. In the search for data relating to the history of the book he was describing, Medina carried on, furthermore, an old custom of Spanish bibliographers, that is, the study of privileges, addresses to the reader, introductions, and other preliminaries. This is incomparably the richest of American bibliographical projects of a general character. It is generous; it might even be said it is prodigal, for in most instances the long quotations from preliminaries, from archival material, or from other books might well have been compressed by the compiler himself into a brief and satisfying statement. The money thus saved in typesetting would probably have enabled him to procure a better paper upon which to print his volumes, for there is a sharp contrast between the intellectual luxury of Medina's books and the undigested wood pulp upon which many of them are printed.

The two examples of subject bibliographies which I have time to mention are the work of living and still active writers. Mr. Henry R. Wagner's *The Spanish Southwest* is very much in the Harrisse tradition. It is a leisurely study, chronologically arranged, of a relatively small number of titles. Full titles are followed by helpful but not expansive collations, which lack precise statement of contents. The emphasis is laid upon the author's commentary. When Mr. Wagner has finished his discussion of a book, there is very little left that one needs to know about it. Drawing upon the book itself, upon the life of the author, upon archival sources, upon general and local secondary historical materials, and upon his own special geographical knowledge, he answers all the questions likely to be asked as to the relationship of a particular text to the events which brought it into being. In doing this he has made his book a work of history rather than simply a catalogue of sources for the historian's use.

The second of the two subject bibliographies I have in mind is the group of three separate books by Thomas J. Holmes which we call "The Mather Bibliography." This work I have acclaimed in the past and still acclaim as a well-nigh perfect application of bibliographical method to the study of history. Mr. Holmes's arrangement of his materials is alphabetical by title, but accompanying each work is a chronological conspectus of the entire output of the author concerned. In these six volumes on Increase, Cotton, and the minor Mathers the title-pages are photographically reproduced, size is stated both by fold of sheet and linear measurement, collations are given by pages and signatures, contents are set forth in full by pages, copies are located, and in each instance the entry is completed by an extensive note of which the subject matter indicates that Mr. Holmes has not only read the book before him but every other book related to it. New England life and thought are illuminated on virtually every page of the Mather trilogy.

This review of certain outstanding American bibliographies of three centuries was begun to provide background for the discussion still to come. More has been done by it than this, however, for gradually as the list extended itself there have emerged from the descriptions of its separate elements certain processes in the organization of materials which seem to have become the normal procedure in the bibliographical treatment of Americana. The chronological arrangement of titles, for example, is seen to have been the mode adopted for most of the important works mentioned. As bibliographical procedure developed, more and more attention was given to the correct transcription of titles and to the correct description of format, and while this change was coming about, emphasis was placed increasingly, through the compiler's commentary, upon the presentation of the book as a text. In the period we have reviewed no uniformity, not even a preferred method, was evolved in the transcription of titles and in the statement of collations. Perhaps there should be no uniformity in these procedures, but after all the world has found that in swimming, running, riding, dancing, even in shaving one's face, the uniformity of practice called "form" is of high importance, the tested way of doing which makes easier routine operations and becomes the springboard of instinctive action in an emergency. Let us think for a while of the validity of "form" in bibliographical procedure.

It is obvious that differences of intention on the part of compilers demand different standards of bibliographical description. Long ago Mr. Pollard said that if you simply wanted to record the fact that a book of a certain title existed, a title-a-line list was sufficient for the purpose. But we are not interested here and now in this simplest form of book listing. What we are seeking is a form which, to put it at the lowest, enables the reader to identify texts, to discriminate between editions, issues, and variant publications of those texts, and to fix the position of a given text in relation to other versions of the same work. At the highest, we seek a form which will do these things and at the same time enable the bibliographer to set before his readers the condition or event or movement which brought that text into being, to record its influence, locate copies of it still in existence, and to describe the history and appearance of the specific copy or copies in the compiler's hands.

Choice between these two possibilities is, of course,

determined by the intention which moves us. If we are making a catalogue of a library or a large private collection or compiling an extensive bibliography of a subject, we must concentrate upon brevity and simplicity. Otherwise the expenditure of time, money, and effort becomes so great and the results attained so small in comparison as to defeat the original purpose of the work. As an intermediate form of entry, assuming the author's name as the first element, the following standard may be suggested:

1. Title in shortened form but full enough to show what the book is about, omitted phrases indicated by three dots, and with no violence done to grammatical construction by the condensation.

2. Compressed imprint, consisting of place, name of printer or publisher, if given, and date in Roman numbers, if so printed.

3. Collation, with size by fold of sheet and a summary statement of signatures, *i.e.*, A-G^8, H^6, unless irregularity requires a detailed statement. Pagination by summary statement, *i.e.*, pages 1-124, unless errors in numbering require some such statement as pages 1-8, 5-8, 1-120.

4. Notes to be employed only when needed to bring out essential bibliographical features.

Here is a form in which technical description is carried far enough to enable one to identify editions and generally to differentiate between issues and variations. Most differences between editions and issues readily reveal themselves in the wording of titles, the places of publication, the changes in the names of publishers or combinations of publishers, in the make-up of the book as indicated by signatures, and in the errors or peculiarities of the pagination as printed. There would be no notes associated with this form of entry except occasionally when needed to establish differences not brought out in title, collation, or imprint. It is obvious that this is not an ideal form of book description, but it is an intelligent one, useful under many conditions in which a more elaborate procedure is inadvisable.

Before taking up the discussion of a bibliographical record more intensively carried through than is possible or desirable in a library catalogue, it may be well to affirm certain generalizations. The first and most important affirmation is that the end of bibliographical analysis is the elucidation of the history of texts. It follows that bibliography is not an end but a means, a process in the study of the transmission of texts. These are accepted definitions. I need not labor to justify the conception of bibliography which they make explicit. There are those, however, who adhere to this conception and still practise something which seems to me to fall short of the fullest and richest use of the procedure it embodies. There are students who record the most careful and intensive studies of the physical characteristics of the book they describe and leave it at that, saying, in effect, that the literary historian must take it on from there. I am convinced that this is not the correct procedure in the case of Americana, nor am I sure that it is correct for books of any kind. In examining bibliographies of modern authors in which a most impressive amount of work has gone toward the search for points, the description of end papers and binding, and binding ornamentation, I feel about as uplifted as if I had been handed the specifications for job Number XXX sent from the editorial office of the publisher to the foreman of the printing shop and the head of the bindery. The final result does not show in what order or in what predetermined combinations the pages and sheets came off the press but in what chance combinations they issued from the stockroom. I realize that these descriptions are helpful to many collectors, but having said that much I stop. In this procedure books are treated simply as objects. There is little to differentiate them from chairs, tables, or houses, and when this occurs with records of the human spirit, either in the description of modern novels or of ancient histories, drought has begun its work upon the bibliographical garden.

In my creed, one has done only half his job when he has completed his description of the *form* in which a text has been presented to the world. From this point onward he is to be, or should be, concerned with the text, with the treasure which the earthen vessel contains; concerned, that is, with the circumstances which brought the text into being; the relationship between circumstances, author, and composition; the publication progress of the book; subsequent editions or issues; or, its passage into oblivion. This is the reality of bibliographical purpose. Henry Stevens of Vermont used to represent Bibliography pictorially as a well from which sprang, green and dripping, the living tree of knowledge. Unless bibliography is practised in the spirit of that conception, it becomes a species of research which closely approaches sterility.

From this point we shall be speaking of what is called "full-dress bibliography," the complete listing and analysis of the literature of a subject, the works of an individual author, the production of a press, the possessions of a private collector or of a small library. The ideal form for such a bibliography, it seems to me, is one which is simple, compact, and comprehensive. The first decision which must be made has to do with the question of the arrangement of titles, whether titles are to be listed in a single alphabet under the names of authors, or in the chronological sequence of their publication.

It has been indicated earlier in this inquiry that the trend of practice among the bibliographers of Americana has been toward the chronological arrangement of titles. The alphabet is a convenience under many conditions. We lisp it in infancy, and thenceforth our lives are built upon and around it, but no one has ever contended that it has a basis in logic. No instrument more effective for the fragmentation of thought could be devised, indeed, than the catalogue arranged upon the alphabetical principle, and, after all, one of the services of bibliography is the organizing of thought for the purpose of synthesis. There is, on the other hand, a sort of cosmic orderliness about chronology, based, as it is, upon the relationship between the earth and the universe or, rather, between the earth and the other bodies of the solar system. As the years and the centuries unroll, great cities flourish and decline, nations rise and fall, and changes occur in the mind and heart of man. That development, either of growth or decay, is recorded by the monuments of art and literature which man leaves behind him. Whether the period set forth in the chronological catalogue be one of a century, or a decade, or a single year, the books published provide a picture of events and of the origin and development of the ideas which in that period have inhibited the people or moved them to action. This picture is at once a still and a movie, according to whether one wants to see the period as a whole or in process of growth. I suppose the principle of chronological arrangement has been most impressively applied in the catalogue of the great Thomason pamphlet collection in the British Museum, in which the pamphlets and books brought out in twenty-two years of violence, indecision, and change, 1640-1661, are arranged under years, and, within the years, actually by months and days. That catalogue becomes in itself a slowly unfolding history of the events and ideas of the Puritan Revolution, for that is exactly the bit of magic which is worked when a group of books on the same general subject is arranged chronologically in the order of publication. Not only does such a catalogue provide source materials in number, but itself as a whole or in chosen groups of years becomes a source for the historian's consideration. Simply to read the titles of Evans's *American Bibliography* for the year 1769 is surely to discover the turbulence of American life and ideas in the period of approaching revolution. Nothing of this comes from the catalogue with titles arranged alphabetically by authors' names. Nor does it come with the same quality of unity from a reading of titles arranged within the neat categories of the *catalogue raisonné*. This has been understood by earlier bibliographers in their treatment of Americana—by White Kennett, Rich, Harrisse, Bartlett, Cole, Medina, and Wagner. The nature of the material arising from a life in which event followed fast upon event, in which there was movement and change, progress toward a greater knowledge, a larger prosperity, a greater enlightenment, almost made it imperative that the material be arranged in such fashion as to leave the line of growth clear to the view.

To speak lightly of Sabin's *Dictionary* is no part of my purpose. Certainly no one can do that who every day of his life takes it up with thankfulness and lays it down with gratitude for service rendered. But one may regret the service it does not perform as well as feel grateful for the answers it gives though careful transcriptions and through the mediation of concise word and symbol. It is a great work of reference to which one goes when he knows the name of the author of a book he is seeking. But one would never go to it for aid in comprehending the life of a period or of a place within a given period. In all probability no one has ever been moved to reflection through an association of ideas set up by a page of Sabin. I went recently to Sabin, for example, to look for a description of Edward Burrough's *A Declaration of the Sad and Great Persecution . . . of the . . . Quakers, in New England*, of London, 1660. Above this title and below it on the Sabin page are, respectively, *The Works of Elihu Burritt: containing 'Sparks from the Anvil,' etc.* of London, 1848, and

C. Burroughs, *Address . . . at the Dedication of the New High School House,* Portsmouth, New Hampshire, 1856. There is nothing in these or in other nearby titles to suggest that Edward Burrough's book was anything more than an object *in vacuo,* but I turn to the current John Carter Brown *Catalogue* and run through the titles for the years 1659 and 1660. There I find that Edward Burrough's book was a single item in a vehement protest against cruelty and intolerance. Preceding it and following it in those years are works by George Fox, Ann Gould, James Nayler, Humphrey Norton, John Rous, George Bishop, Francis Howgill, Isaac Penington, Marmaduke Stephenson, and other writers of the Society of Friends as well as replies to these by anti-Quaker controversialists and officials of the government of Massachusetts. A glance at these titles is enough to show that here was a tense moment in history, that blood had been spilled in New England and was crying from the ground for vengeance. There is no doubt that the clamor raised by the English Quakers in this emergency had its place in the development of ideas and conduct in England and America. Nowhere is the force and extent of this clamor so emphatically brought to the consciousness as in a chronological listing of titles for the years concerned—certainly not in Sabin, and not in Joseph Smith's alphabetically arranged *Descriptive Catalogue of Friends' Books.*

Early in this discussion it was said that though Americana did not require a form of entry fundamentally different from that employed in the description of works of literature it nevertheless seemed through its nature to demand a shift of emphasis within that form. This statement must now be defined and expanded.

The tendency today among learned bibliographers is toward the elaboration of technical bibliographical procedures. A normal entry for a work of early literature comprises under their hands a title transcription in which the several type faces and other typographical features of the title-page have been reproduced, an elaborate collation by signatures, a collation by contents in which the heading of every section is exactly transcribed, and a note in which the further information conveyed to the reader is technical in character. This, we may say, is the accepted bibliographical standard built up through two generations of serious study and practice by the bibliographers of England and America. When I say that in the treatment of Americana a shift of emphasis must occur, I mean that emphasis must be removed from this minutely exact transcription and elaborate physical description of the book and placed upon a commentary resulting from research into textual history and relationships.

Works of the creative imagination—plays, poems, and novels—are subjective in origin, proceeding from within, from the mind and spiritual experience of the author. The normal work of Americana, on the other hand, is an objective work, brought into being through the impact upon the author of some event or movement or set of circumstances outside himself. In many instances the book so produced becomes an agency which bears its part in the further development of that movement, or becomes an element integrated with the history of the event of which it treats. The relationship of book to event or to other books treating directly or inferentially the same subject becomes a matter of interest to the historian, and the bibliographer with a sensitive feeling for these relationships will endeavor to answer for himself and his readers certain questions about the book he is describing. He will try to determine the impelling force behind the creation of his text, the circumstances of its composition, and the conditions of publication by means of which this force was given effective and enduring body as a printed book. He will discover and make reference to other editions as a measure of the esteem in which the book was held by its author's contemporaries, regardless, let it be said emphatically, of what we think of it today; regardless, that is, of evaluation or literary criticism. He will examine those other editions for textual revisions or changes, additions, or omissions. He will, in short, endeavor to discover all he can about the text before him, regarding it as a living force brought into being by the contacts of men and ideas, by man's conflict with nature and with the intellectual considerations of his time.

Here, in broad outline, is the shift of emphasis of which I have spoken, a shift from elaboration in the description of the physical form of a book to the consideration of its meaning in relation to its time and subject. It is sometimes objected that in making this shift the author becomes literary historian rather than bibliographer, that he goes beyond the function of the bibliographer. I do not know that I have a categorical reply to that objection, but I believe that through seeking always in our analysis of books for their significance in relation to life we make the most satisfactory approach to the hurly-burly, the disorder, the vitality, and the profound meaning of the field of letters we call Americana.

Two instances in my recent experience explain clearly the service rendered the student of history by the search for the significance of texts about which I have been speaking. For many years the John Carter Brown Library has owned a book without title-page, long since identified as *A List of Copies of Charters, from the Commissioners for Trade and Plantations, Presented to the Honourable the House of Commons . . . London: Printed in the Year M.DCC.XLI.* A few weeks ago the Library acquired a copy with title-page, which came to us with no comment from its former owner beyond the phrase "privately printed" in explanation of the brevity of its imprint. I find that title in several bibliographies and catalogues, but in none of them is it so described as to give sustenance to the historian. In one of my favorite catalogues the title-page is reproduced in photographic facsimile, the name of the author is given (though given incorrectly), there are a full collation by signatures, a full collation by contents, linear measurements both by inches and centimeters, a description of the binding of the copy described, and a brief note referring to its relationship to the succeeding entry. The compiler who entered the book in this fashion, with comprehensive physical description, leaves it right there with all the questions raised by the title-page unanswered, such questions as what was the House of Com-

mons petition there referred to, what was the relationship of the Commissioners of Trade to the book, and,
above all, why and by whom were six American colonial
charters collected and published in London in the un-
exciting and featureless year of 1741. It may be said that
it is enough for the historian that the bibliographer
should let him know that this book exists and what it
contains; that it is the historian's function to answer the
questions it poses; in brief, it may be said and has been
said, let the historian cook his own meat. I believe that
to be the wrong attitude for two reasons. The first is
that most historians won't bother. They are not interested in bibliography. For all that they may do about it,
the meat will lie there in the deep-freeze compartment
until the end of time. The other reason I have already
given, that is, my high conception of the function of
the bibliographer, his duty to display the significance of
his wares.

In the instance cited, it proves to be a relatively simple
task, with nothing of the recondite about it, to increase
the potential importance of this book in the eyes of the
historian. Reference to the *Journal of the Commissioners for Trade and Plantations* and to the *Votes of the
House of Commons* enables one to trace the history of
the compilation of this book from a petition of the
House asking that his Majesty require the Lords of
Trade to make this collection of charters, through its
presentation to the House by the Commissioners of
Trade, and, finally, to the House's order to print it. In
the course of this examination of the record it comes out
that the purpose of the collection was to serve as a basic

document in the Parliamentary investigation of the right, implied or expressed, of the individual colonies to issue paper money. For the historian this purely legal collection has thus become a document in one of the enduring problems of American political and economic life and British imperial administration. No definite answer is given by the records consulted as to who printed the book, though it could be suggested on typographical grounds that it was the work of John Baskett, the King's printer, nor is it clear why each charter has its own separate pagination and signatures unless it was intended that they be issued separately as well as in combination. It does not appear, furthermore, whether the original John Carter Brown copy on thick paper was one of an issue without title-page intended for members of the House while the newly acquired thin-paper copy with title-page was one of an issue intended for general distribution. Though all questions are not answered by this brief research, enough has been done to show that our dull legal collection described as "privately printed" was an official publication of the House of Commons issued in connection with a fifty-year-old and, at that time, still unsolved problem of colonial American politics and economy.

The second instance I want to bring to your attention is one in which a publication about an American colony clearly relates the affairs of that colony to the large considerations of world politics. We learn from the *Diary of the First Earl of Egmont* that in January 1741 the Trustees of Georgia ordered Benjamin Martyn, their secretary, to prepare "An Account shewing the

Progress of the Colony of Georgia." Thenceforth we follow in the Egmont *Diary* and in the *Votes of the House of Commons* the curious history of this book. We learn, for example, that it was not a publication of the Trustees, as sometimes assumed, but that on February 26, 1740/41 the Commons ordered that such a number of the "Account" be printed "as shall be sufficient for the Use of the Members of the House." Thereafter a strong effort on the part of the Georgia supporters in Parliament to bring the matter of this "Account" to debate was countered by their opponents with a summary adjournment of the session when the debate seemed imminent. Finally we read the conclusion of Egmont that Sir Robert Walpole was afraid to let that debate occur lest as the result of it Georgia be declared useful to England and Sir Robert's Government be unable to turn the colony over to Spain or abandon it as a concession to the Spanish in the treaty about to be made.

This investigation shows, as does that of *A List of Copies of Charters*, how illuminating is that bibliographical process which seeks to determine the reason for publication as part of the history of a text. Instead of the usual piece of promotion literature, this book is seen to be a weapon, and an effective weapon in the Georgia Trustees' offensive against Walpole's indifference to the fate of their great patriotic and philanthropic project. To win in this offensive by default left Egmont and, presumably, his fellow trustees, dissatisfied. They had hoped that through a parliamentary debate would come justification of their own administration and a clear statement of the value of Georgia to England.

The three main elements upon which should be based a bibliographical standard for Americana have been brought out separately in the foregoing discussion and are now before us for integration. These are the chronological arrangement of titles, transcription and description sufficiently detailed to make possible differentiation between texts, and commentary upon the history and transmission of the texts themselves. The practical application of these principles permits great latitude of choice. Large books have been and are being written about the transcription of titles and the infinitude of printers' practices, operations, and shop accidents which may be expressed in the collation. The consideration of editions, issues, variants, mixed copies, sub-variants, and other intricacies of the sort forms a literature in itself. I assume that this time and place are unsuitable for the detailed discussion of all these refinements of practice, but briefly we may consider for a moment a skeleton of the standard form of entry toward which I have been leading. I present this standard without dogmatic intent as to details of practice, saying only it seems to me that to do less than the form suggests is to fall short of a comprehensive statement, while to do more is to introduce unnecessary complications. The standard I propose is as follows:

1. Author's name.
2. Photographic reproduction of title-page if possible, but if not, full or adequate transcription of title and imprint with line endings, with omissions, if any, indicated, but without effort to differentiate between type faces or the several kinds of

    rules, ornaments, and borders found upon the page.

3. Collation by fold of sheet with summary statement of signatures, number of leaves, and statement of pagination as actually printed.
4. Collation of contents by inclusive pages.
5. Linear measurements.
6. Note embodying the history and significance of the text as outlined earlier in the present discussion.
7. References.
8. Location of copies.

I am aware that in certain features of this suggested form, such as the simplified transcription of title and the summary collation by signatures, I have proposed a minimum not altogether acceptable to many careful bibliographers of today. It is not that I fail in respect for their concern in a greater and greater refinement of procedure. Now and then, too rarely for my own satisfaction, I have carried through a minute analysis of the make-up of a book. There are few tasks more exacting, more demanding of sustained reflection and of the exercise of the constructive imagination. But it has been my experience that in the treatment of Americana the reward of this procedure seldom compensates for the pains required to carry it through.

The historian is less interested in minor textual differences than is the student of literature. Such differences often are important, but the cost of discovering them and making them known is immense when it may be achieved only by the most intensive physical analysis of a volume; by transcribing a title in such manner as to show the several type faces employed by its printer; by recording and describing in the transcription every rule, double rule, printer's ornament, or border; by reproducing in full the text of the title, including long quotations from Holy Writ or the classics; and finally, with even greater labor, by making a minute analysis of signatures, headlines, and catchwords, in order to discover, among other things, how many presses were employed in the printing and what pages were printed at the same time from the same form. Extraordinary results have been attained in the field of letters through this sort of bibliographical procedure, for in creative writing every textual difference, whether a radical revision or simply the change of an adjective or the cadence of a line, is or may be important to the student of taste or feeling. But I repeat that in my experience with Americana the discoveries made by these exhaustive procedures are so seldom important as to make their general adoption of no avail. Better to use that physical effort and cerebration in the study of the history and significance of the text in its relationship to subject and to other texts.

There is nothing new in what I have said. It has been my privilege merely to trace the descent of a traditional method and to seek a rational explanation for its existence. Long ago, Harrisse, in the introduction to his *Bibliotheca Americana Vetustissima,* said all that was needed about the function of the commentary in the bibliographical description of Americana. Nearly forty years ago in the appendix of an article, *Some Points in*

Bibliographical Descriptions, by Alfred W. Pollard and W. W. Greg, Mr. Pollard suggested the concise, compact styles of transcription and physical description which I have been advocating. Progress is not made by leaps but by the carrying on of tradition, the intelligent carrying on of tradition, in the course of which the less desirable procedure is discarded, the tried and tested is retained and improved, and the new and experimentally successful is given trial. In the specific instance before us we have arrived at a standard by discarding full and typographically exact transcriptions in favor of simple transcriptions in one face of type, by substituting for the terse collations of our predecessors a description which shows how the physical book was planned and carried through by its printer, and by placing special emphasis upon notes which provide elucidation of the history of texts, a practice derived from a philosophical consideration of the material of our special concern. Here is a standard which has been formed not by one man or by a society, but by the reaction of three centuries of bibliographers in contact with the printed material we call Americana.